MW01625288

Talking About Abortion

First Edition

Names, characters, places and incidents are products of the author's imagination or are used fictitiously and are not to be construed as real.

ISBN-13: 9780578390864

ISBN-10: 0578390868

Published by
Sidgwick Press

Talking About Abortion

An American Dialogue

by James DeHullu

DEDICATION

The English philosopher John Stuart Mill (1806-1873) was raised to be a follower of the social reformer Jeremy Bentham. As time went on, however, he came to believe that Bentham's philosophy was inadequate. Something more was needed. Mill read widely and concluded that there was an element of truth in many of the philosophies he encountered. He hoped to formulate a new synthesis of existing ideas that would be widely accepted. His success was limited, but his insight and his hope were noble. This book is dedicated to him.

TABLE OF CONTENTS

PREFACE

This book is the sequel to my previous book *What Americans Believe*. In the previous book I created a set of characters who discussed several broad frameworks of ideas for thinking about American politics. In this one, many of those same characters discuss a narrower set of questions concerning one specific moral and political problem – the problem of abortion.

There are few issues in the politics of the last 50 years that have generated the passion that surrounds abortion. Praised as a fundamental right by some and decried as murder by others, it has no emotional equal. Issues such as race, gay rights, gender, immigration, and income inequality fail to match the intensity of the abortion debate.

This book presents a dialogue on some of the moral and legal issues related to abortion. Hopefully, the characters present the views most popular among Americans. Nevertheless, its purpose is not to argue for or against any of those views. If it helps readers to better understand the views that others hold and introduces them to a sample of the philosophical literature on the subject, it will have been successful. If it helps some readers to develop a reasoned position of their own on the issues, so much the better.

Jim DeHullu

Philadelphia, 2022

1. INTRODUCTION

Talking About Abortion is a dialogue among several fictitious American students interested in moral and political philosophy. Their main subject is the morality of abortion. In other words, they wish to discuss when, if ever, abortion is morally permissible or prohibited. They are also interested in a number of legal questions related to abortion. The discussion is guided by two fictitious college professors named Sidgwick and Conway. Both are named after historical figures – the Victorian philosopher Henry Sidgwick and the 17th-century philosopher Lady Anne Conway.

The participants take a variety of positions on the moral and legal questions they discuss.

- Readers can follow the main argument of the dialogue by reading the speakers identified with the letters **MP** ("Main Path"). The images of Sidgwick and Conway are highlighted when they speak on the main path.

- Speakers who make comments on the main argument are identified with the letters **OP** ("Off Path"). Comments add clarity, detail, or responses to the main argument. They are shaded with solid gray and italicized for easy identification.

The dialogue has five parts: an introduction to the issues and the characters in the dialogue; a discussion of personhood and moral rights; arguments for and against the morality of abortion; a discussion of abortion and the law; and, finally, a short conclusion in which the characters sum up their views.

The dialogue does not present final answers to hotly contested questions. The goal is not to supply those answers, but rather to introduce concepts, claims, and arguments that are relevant to the issues. In the end, the reader must decide which concepts, which claims, and which arguments are most compelling.

Professor Sidgwick Speaking

WELCOME

Good morning and thank you for coming. I'm looking forward to today's discussion.

Some of you know me, but others do not. I teach philosophy here at the university. My courses focus on moral and political philosophy. I have a special interest in modern liberalism – especially the philosophy of John Rawls – and I sometimes lead a graduate seminar on justice.

I have asked Professor Conway to join us today. She has been interested in questions about abortion for many years. Her perspective may be helpful because she has studied both moral philosophy and law.

Before Professor Conway introduces herself, I would like to clarify the questions we are focused on in this colloquium.

Since the Supreme Court decided *Roe v. Wade* in 1973, Americans have argued passionately about whether and when abortion is morally permissible. They have also debated various legal and constitutional questions related to abortion, including when it should be legal and whether there is a constitutional right to end a pregnancy. We are going to focus on the moral question: When, if ever, is abortion morally permissible or impermissible? We will also briefly discuss several legal questions.

Professor Conway and I are not here to give you answers to these questions. Our goal is to facilitate a discussion. In the end, you must come to your own conclusions. Now, let me turn it over to Professor Conway.

Professor Conway Speaking

MP WELCOME

Good morning. It's good to be here. This is the first time that Professor Sidgwick and I have worked together to facilitate a discussion like this. I hope that it will prove interesting and useful for all of us.

Like Professor Sidgwick, I have an appointment in the Department of Philosophy, but I have also studied and written about a number of legal issues. I realize that this is a class for students in the philosophy and political science departments, but I hope that I can introduce some legal questions that you will find intriguing.

Professor Sidgwick has asked Ayesha to talk with each of you and to give us a brief description of where you stand philosophically and what you think about abortion at this time. I say "at this time" because it's possible that some of you will change your views in the course of this discussion. Let's try to be open to that possibility.

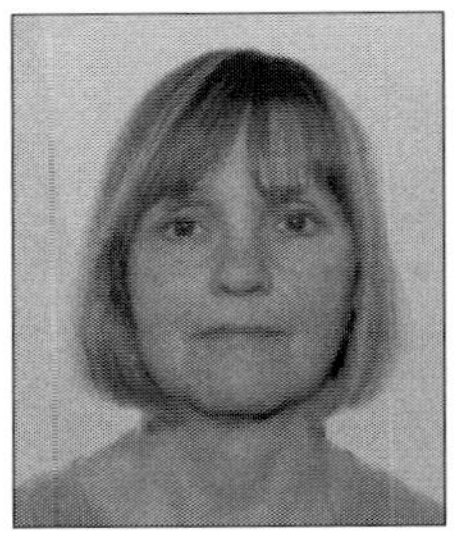

Professor Conway Speaking

OP COMMENT ON OUR QUESTIONS

I want you to notice how Professor Sidgwick has phrased our main moral question. He has asked whether and when abortion is morally permissible or prohibited. That is the way Americans usually state the issue.

I want to remind you that that is not the only way to frame moral issues. Philosophers commonly distinguish between the right (or sometimes rights) and the good. Those are two different ways of talking about morality. The right is generally opposed to what is wrong. It is usually a categorical judgment, and it usually appeals to some set of rules that apply to a situation. The good is generally opposed to the bad. It is on a continuum of better and worse, and it usually depends on the consequences of our actions.

It is quite possible for someone to have a right to do something, but it is not good (or best) to do that thing. It is also possible for something to be good, but we have no right to do it because it would violate the applicable rules.

In the case of abortion, for example, it may be that a particular woman has a moral right to have an abortion, but it would not be good (or best) for her to do so. Perhaps it would ruin her marriage or have some other undesirable consequence.

My point is that right now we are not asking whether having an abortion is a good thing or the best thing to do. We are asking whether and when it is right or wrong. Asking about the good can open up new considerations that you may want to think about.

Professor Sidgwick Speaking

OP COMMENT ON THE DEBATE ON ABORTION

Much of the talk about a woman's right to control her body or an unborn child's right to life is made up of clichés and slogans. There are also powerful images used at rallies and demonstrations. One side carries pictures of coat hangers. The other side carries pictures of dismembered fetuses.

Slogans and images may be politically useful and may give us a way to express strong feelings. Nevertheless, they do not offer the nuts and bolts of a reasoned argument.

We all use slogans at times, but we need to dig deeper and think more precisely about what we are saying, why we believe it, and how to answer critics. If we avoid the digging, we allow the slogans to do our thinking for us. In a famous essay, George Orwell once warned that if we give ourselves to the slogans or the jargon of any political group, we are abandoning the intellectual process itself. Besides that, slogans sometimes give the illusion of deep understanding and thoughtful answers where there are none.

Today, let's try to develop clear, well-argued positions, and see where that approach leads us.

Ayesha Speaking

INTRODUCTIONS

I want to introduce everyone by giving a short description of their overall political philosophy and their views on abortion.

Dee describes herself as a right-libertarian. She believes in self-ownership and strong individual rights. In her view, we should have minimal government that protects our rights, defends the nation, and enforces contracts. Based on her concept of self-ownership, she believes that women have a moral right to end a pregnancy. She supports very liberal laws on abortion.

Ann is a utilitarian. She believes that moral judgments should be made, and governmental policies should be chosen, in order to maximize human welfare. She also believes that early abortions are morally permissible and supports moderately liberal abortion laws.

Fred considers himself to be a typical American conservative. He believes in a strict interpretation of the Constitution, a less intrusive federal government, more power to the states, lower taxes, and relatively free markets. He is a Roman Catholic and is morally opposed to nearly all abortions. In his view, the law on abortion is a matter for state governments to decide.

John is not easy to classify politically, but he believes that we should create a society in which everyone has the freedom and resources to develop his or her capacities. He is undecided about some of the philosophical questions related to abortion, but leans toward moderately liberal laws on the subject.

Vera is a committed feminist. She believes that women's interests and women's experiences should have more weight in political affairs. In her view, whether to have an abortion is something for individual women to decide. The law should respect their moral right to make that decision.

Diego is an Evangelical Christian. He bases his moral and political views on his understanding of Christian principles. His emphasis is on stopping the moral decline of our society and the weakening of the family. He believes that most abortions are morally wrong and favors strong laws restricting abortion.

As for me, I'm Ayesha, and like Fred, I'm a Catholic. I have been impressed by 20th-century Catholic social thought. I believe that many abortions are morally wrong, but I wonder whether some early abortions may be permissible. I am undecided about how the law should deal with the issue.

Professor Sidgwick Speaking

MP A NETWORK OF ISSUES

Before we begin the discussion, I would like to be clear that in my view the morality of abortion is not a simple question. The issues are complex, and competent moral philosophers reach different conclusions. The same is true for the legal and constitutional issues. Intelligent, well-informed people differ on these issues. We need to keep that in mind.

There are many philosophical issues connected with abortion, all of which form a conceptual network with logical links. Because of the logical links, the positions we take on one set of issues have implications for the positions we take on others.

Some issues have to do with the nature of persons. Others have to do with moral rights and moral status. Finally, there are questions about government and law.

Let's start by talking about the concept of a person and then go on to discuss the morality of abortion.

Professor Sidgwick Speaking

COMMENT ON A NETWORK OF ISSUES

I want to give you a better idea of the many issues surrounding abortion. Here are some examples:

- *One set of issues concerns the concept of a moral person. For example — What is a moral person? Must a moral person be a human being? Is an embryo a moral person? Is an infant? When does a moral person begin to exist? Can we know? How does personhood connect with the morality of abortion?*

- *Another set concerns the concept of a moral right. For example — What sorts of beings can have rights? Only persons? Can a fetus have rights? A child with severe intellectual disabilities? A whale? An intelligent being from Mars? Which of these can have a right to life? What would such a right imply?*

- *A third set concerns our moral right to control our bodies. For example — How extensive a right does a woman have to control her body and her capacity to reproduce? If an unborn child or fetus has rights, how do they relate to those of its mother?*

- *A final set concerns government and law. For example — Should government remain neutral in moral disputes? Should it support the mother's freedom if experts disagree about the moral status of the fetus? Should it protect the fetus because it is helpless and innocent? Do laws against abortion violate the constitutional ban on establishing a religion? Is there a constitutional right to privacy that includes the right to abort a pregnancy? Did the Supreme Court overreach in deciding* Roe v. Wade*? How should the law respond to the moral and religious diversity of our society?*

How do we approach and answer questions like these? Are there rational methods for doing so or simply brute assertions? What if we are uncertain about some of the answers? Those are all questions to consider.

We could also ask about the rights of fathers. I'm going to suggest that we leave those out of our discussion today because most writers focus on the mother and her child.

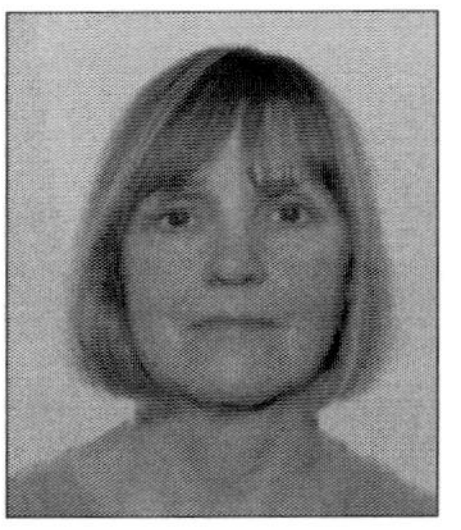

Professor Conway Speaking

OP COMMENT ON HUMANS, PERSONS, AND MORAL STATUS

Some writers believe that when discussing the morality of abortion, the crucial question is whether the embryo or the fetus is alive, whether it is human, or whether it possesses human life. In defense of their answers, they often describe the complex physical structure of the embryo, its genetic makeup, and the similarity of the late-term fetus to an infant. Other writers believe that those questions do not capture the main issue with which we are concerned. They agree that the embryo is alive, that it is a human embryo, and that it is a form of human life, but they claim that the dispute is not about those biological issues. Instead, they believe that the main question concerns the moral status of the embryo or the fetus. To get at that issue, they believe we must talk about personhood, values, and individual moral rights.

2. PERSONS AND RIGHTS

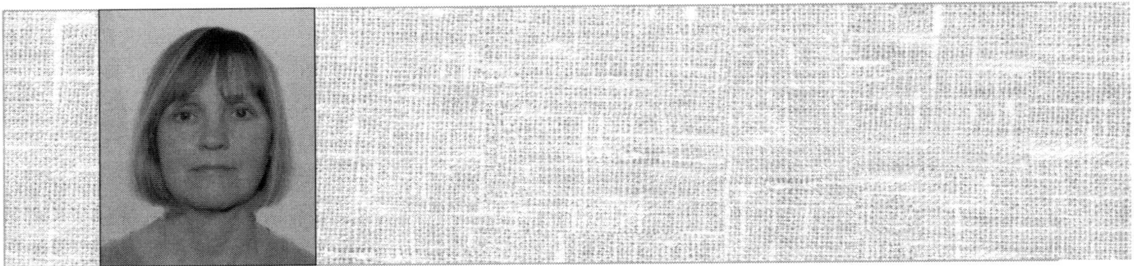

Professor Conway Speaking

MP PERSONS

Professor Sidgwick and I decided to start with questions about the concept of a person because many people consider personhood the pivotal issue. If the embryo (or the fetus or the unborn child) is a person, they conclude that abortion is (or is usually) on a par with homicide. If not, they conclude that it is a far less serious matter, perhaps only a matter of prudence and personal choice.

This approach focuses on the nature and moral status of the embryo or fetus, but it is not the only approach to questions about the morality of abortion. Some writers, such as philosophers Rosalind Hursthouse and Loren Lomasky, believe that the moral status of the embryo or the fetus is irrelevant to our main moral question. Others focus on the rights and welfare of women or the overall good of society.

Eventually, however, most philosophical discussion considers questions about personhood, even if only to downgrade their importance. We will begin with those questions, bearing in mind that there are other approaches that we could take.

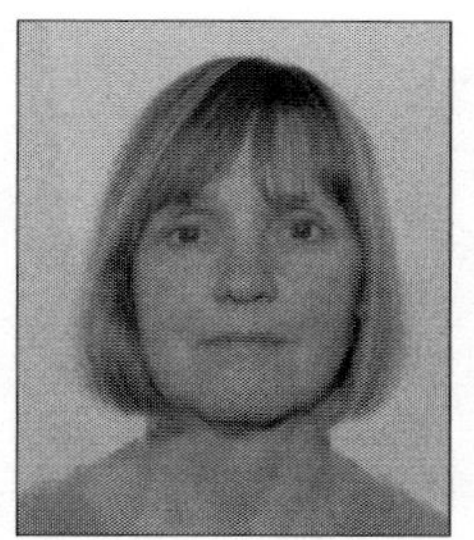

Professor Conway Speaking

COMMENT ON TERMINOLOGY

By the way, I suggest that we use the word 'embryo' to refer to the child in the earliest stage of pregnancy, roughly the first eight weeks, and the word 'fetus' to refer to it in the later stages. Sometimes people disagree about the exact meaning of those terms, but the details usually won't matter for our purposes. If they do matter at some point, we can say so.

Another term you may find useful is 'moral community.' I take that to refer to the whole collection of beings that deserve consideration when moral decisions are made. Moral decisions are usually concerned with whether actions are right or wrong, good or bad. They usually involve deciding what someone should or should not do. The moral community definitely includes adult human beings, but what else does it include? Does it include animals, embryos, or infants? Those are complicated questions.

Professor Sidgwick Speaking

MP WHAT IS A MORAL PERSON?

It is important to ask how we should define the concept of a person, why persons have a high moral status, and how that status connects with the morality of abortion. Those are tough questions. And remember this: We want more than a description of how the word 'person' is ordinarily used or a list of the physical or psychological characteristics of typical persons. We are trying to get at the concept of a *moral* person – a being that has the highest moral status including the strongest right to life. What must such a person be like? Who or what qualifies?

By the way, I suggest that from here on, when we refer to persons, it will be to *moral* persons unless otherwise stated. You can add the word 'moral' as a reminder if you wish.

Dee Speaking

MP CLARIFICATION

I just want to be clear about what we are doing. We aren't just trying to describe what we ordinarily call a person. We're trying to decide what qualities make someone or something a *moral* person.

A minimal definition of a moral person tells us that moral persons have the same moral status, including the same moral rights, as an adult like any of us. Its rights might include, for example, a right to liberty, a right not to be tortured, or a right not to be assaulted or killed.

For our discussion, we want more than a minimal definition. We are looking for an *expanded* definition that specifies the qualities that give persons a very high moral status.

The hope is that if we can figure out what makes someone a moral person, it will help us to decide when, if ever, abortion is morally acceptable.

I think I get it.

Professor Conway Speaking

MP PERSONS

I would like to make two comments before you start proposing definitions.

First, keep in mind that it won't help to arbitrarily define 'person' in a way that supports your views on abortion. You must be able to supply *reasons* why others should accept your definition. Once you have done that, you could try to decide whether the embryo or the fetus qualifies as a person.

Second, we should understand that even if we were to adopt a specific definition of a person, and even if we agreed that the embryo or the fetus is a person, it may not settle our main question. That is because the embryo or the fetus would not be the only person involved in the case of abortion. The mother is also a person, and we all agree that she has a full set of moral rights including a strong right to life. She may also have a greater or lesser degree of responsibility for becoming pregnant or remaining pregnant. A final conclusion about abortion must consider the interests, claims, and rights of both the fetus and the mother. Her responsibility for her pregnancy may also enter into our thinking.

John Speaking

MP PERSONS

I'll be honest with you. I'm not sure how to define 'moral person.' Professor Sidgwick said that we are trying to describe the sort of thing that has a high moral status, a being that has a full set of moral rights or at least a strong right to life. But what counts? We all agree on some cases in which something is a person and other cases in which it is not. But how do we go from there to a useful definition of a 'moral person' or 'moral personhood'? I made up a list of features that we might use to specify what makes someone or something a moral person. Here it is:

- Having human parents
- Having 46 human chromosomes
- Being alive and conscious
- Being able to experience pleasure and pain
- Exhibiting certain kinds of brain activity
- Having wants, needs, and purposes
- Having interests that can be protected or thwarted
- Being self-conscious or conscious of oneself as a subject or as an enduring being with a past and a future
- Being able to reason in fairly complex ways
- Being able to use language
- Having memories connected with oneself and knowing it
- Being able to think about one's life as a whole and plan it
- Having a soul
- Being made in the image of God
- Having the potential to develop all or some of the above characteristics

Does this list help? We could use some of these characteristics to specify what makes something a moral person, but which characteristics are relevant? Why should we use some characteristics rather than others? How do we avoid being arbitrary or simply rigging the definition so that it supports our views on abortion? I have to tell you guys, I think this is confusing.

Professor Sidgwick Speaking

MP CHOOSING A DEFINITION

John is right. There are lots of characteristics that we might use to construct an expanded definition of moral personhood.

Philosophers have proposed both narrow and broad definitions. Let's look at some examples and see if that helps.

Vera is going to present a narrow definition that she thinks is plausible. Ayesha, Ann, and Diego will present broader definitions. Later on, we can connect these definitions to our ideas about the morality of abortion.

Vera Speaking

PERSON: A NARROW DEFINITION

OK. I'll take a stab at a definition. But first, full disclosure. My political goal is total equality for women. If I have a bias, that's it. I don't hide it any more than Diego hides his evangelical Christianity. And, by the way, if anybody wants to know, I'm an agnostic as far as religion goes. I don't know whether there's a god or what god thinks about abortion.

Now, let's talk about a definition. Philosopher Mary Ann Warren has argued for very high standards of personhood and so her concept of a person is a narrow one. She believes that the traits most "central" to being a person include consciousness, reasoning, self-motivated activity, the capacity to communicate, and having self-awareness or a self-concept. Those are all high-level cognitive functions, so we could call her definition a cognitive definition (Feinberg anthology, 111-112).

I like Warren's approach because she separates personhood (a moral status) from species membership (a biological or genetic fact). In other words, she separates the moral sense from the genetic sense of 'human.' She grants that the full possession of personhood and a right to life may develop gradually, but it is the traits I have listed that count when determining the degree of that development. In her view, biological facts such as the number of chromosomes or the presence of a heartbeat are not defining qualities. Finally, she tells us that the moral community Professor Conway referred to consists of "all and only people" (Feinberg anthology, 110-111).

I think that Warren has identified the qualities that we value in everyday people. Those are the qualities we hope to protect when we ascribe moral rights to people, and that's why they tell us what makes them moral persons.

Vera Speaking

COMMENT ON WARREN'S DEFINITION

Warren also discounts potential personhood in favor of the actual manifestation of the traits I mentioned. I personally don't think that potential personhood should count anywhere near as much as actual personhood. After all, a potential voter isn't a voter and doesn't have the right to vote. Likewise, a potential person isn't an actual person and doesn't have the rights of a person. If a potential person does have rights, they are outweighed by the rights of a fully developed person when there is a conflict.

John Speaking

COMMENT ON POTENTIAL PERSONS

Vera, I agree that a potential person doesn't automatically have the moral status or the moral rights of a person. But that doesn't mean that it has no moral status or no moral rights at all.

Fred Speaking

COMMENT ON THE NARROW DEFINITION

I agree that being conscious, using reason, having a self-concept, and so on are sufficient conditions for personhood. But are they necessary conditions? I doubt that, and that's the big question.

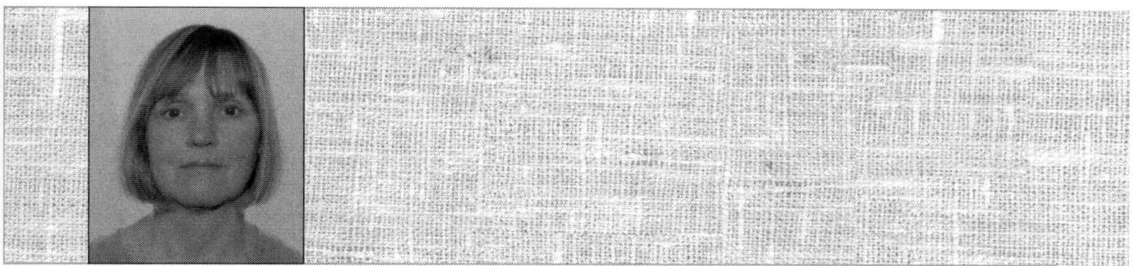

Professor Conway Speaking

MP QUESTIONS TO CONSIDER

Vera's definition raises lots of questions for us to think about.

If having consciousness, intelligence, self-knowledge, and so forth are essential to being a moral person, what about people who have these things to a much higher or a much lower degree than most of us? Do they have a higher or lower moral status than others? Did Einstein have a stronger right to life (or a different set of moral rights) than you or me? Does a great artist like Picasso or a great spiritual leader like Gandhi? What does Vera's definition imply for the rights of those with intellectual disabilities? What about people who lose those characteristics because of injury or old age? What about infants or people in comas?

If you want to develop your views on personhood in a systematic way, give those questions some thought.

Now let's move on to other possible definitions of personhood. Ayesha, you're up.

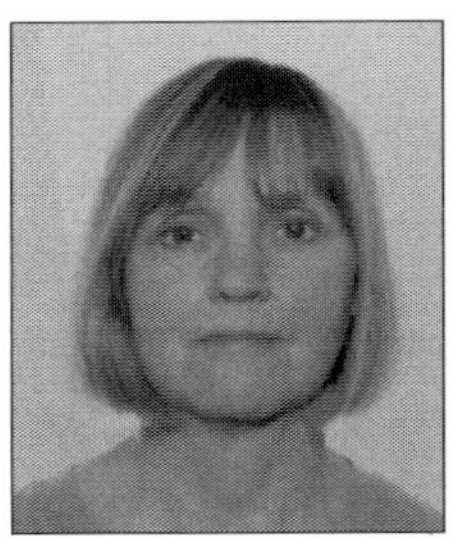

Professor Conway Speaking

OP COMMENT ON THE MORAL COMMUNITY

A few minutes ago, I defined the moral community as all of the beings that ought to be considered when moral decisions are made. That definition leads to more questions. Are all members of the moral community on the same level or are they on different levels? For example, are animals, infants, persons with intellectual disabilities, average people, and Einstein on the same level or are they on different levels with a different moral status or different rights and obligations?

Here's one possible hierarchy. Level I: Beings such as normal adults with a full set of moral rights and duties. They can also be held responsible for what they do. Level II: Beings such as very young children with rights but no duties. They cannot be held responsible for what they do. Level III: Animals such as dogs that may or may not have rights. They have no duties, but it is still wrong to treat them in certain ways. And finally, there are non-members such as rocks that are outside the moral community altogether.

If those levels seem plausible to you, ask yourself what it is that puts adults, young children, animals and so forth on different levels.

Ayesha Speaking

m P PERSON: A BROADER DEFINITION

I believe that Vera's definition has problems. I think Diego is going to talk about that. Right now, I want to offer a definition of personhood that is broader than hers. Philosopher Baruch Brody attempted to specify criteria for being a "human being." By that he meant "a member of the species Homo sapiens who has a right to life similar to the right to life had by you, me, and so on" (Brody 1975, 3).

Brody argued that human beings have some properties that are essential to being human. If a human being loses one of those properties, he or she ceases to be human.

Brody looked at the way we define death as the key to identifying those essential properties – for in defining death we are asking what constitutes the loss of our humanity. Such symptoms as irreversible loss of heart and brain functions are useful criteria of death. Therefore, he concluded, the emergence of a functioning heart and brain is the mark of an emerging human being or person. I'm simplifying a little here, but it seems to me that brain activity was the most important thing to Brody (Brody 1975, 110-114).

Brody's definition of a human being is broader than Vera's definition of personhood because it doesn't require any of the higher cognitive functions like reasoning or having a self-concept.

Dee Speaking

MP REPLY TO AYESHA

I'm not sure why we should believe that brain and heart functions are useful criteria of moral personhood. I agree that their loss marks the death of an organism, but I think that the *person* is gone when the higher brain functions are irreversibly lost. If we take that view, and use a logic similar to Brody's, personhood only begins when those higher brain functions emerge.

Ann Speaking

MP MORAL STANDING: A MODERATE VIEW

I want to rephrase our question and ask what sorts of things have moral standing, rather than asking for a definition of 'moral person.' Something has moral standing if it deserves to be considered when moral decisions are made. In other words, if it is a member of the moral community that Professor Conway mentioned.

I'm going to follow the philosopher L. W. Sumner here. He rejects the claim that rationality is a necessary condition for moral standing. As a result, he would reject Vera's definition of personhood as way too narrow. Instead, he proposes that "sentience" is the proper criterion for moral standing. At a minimum, sentience requires the capacity to feel pleasure and pain. For that reason, a sentient being can be harmed or benefitted. Therefore, it can have rights and it deserves to be considered when moral decisions are made.

Sumner defines sentience broadly. It includes consciousness, feeling, affect, and the capacity to experience pleasure and pain. Because sentience is a matter of degree, different beings can have a higher or lower moral standing than others. A fully developed person has the highest moral standing and strongest right to life (Feinberg anthology, 74).

Moral standing based on sentience encompasses a larger group than Vera's definition of personhood but a smaller group than Brody's definition of human being. It's a middle-of-the-road view.

Diego Speaking

MP PERSON: THE MOST INCLUSIVE DEFINITION

I want to be more inclusive than any of you. Some philosophers offer broader definitions than Warren, Brody, and Sumner. Robert Joyce, a Catholic philosopher, argued that "Every living individual being with the natural potential, as a whole, for knowing, willing, desiring, and relating to others in a self-reflective way is a person" (Joyce 1978, 97). For Joyce, "a person is a being who *can become* aware of his own existence; he can say 'I'" (Joyce and Joyce 1970, 25).

The important thing is potential rather than any actual function. I'll say more about that later.

Let me add something else. A useful definition of personhood has to be clear and verifiable. Ideally, it should be supported by the latest science. The best definition, from a scientific point of view, defines a person or a human being as an organism with 46 human chromosomes. That's a broad definition, and it fits with what Joyce proposed. It also fits my understanding of holy scripture.

Dee Speaking

OP COMMENT ON THE GENETIC DEFINITION

Diego, let me say something about your scientific definition. We all agree that the embryo has 46 human chromosomes, just like an adult person. But the question is whether that is a good reason to believe that the embryo has the same moral status as an adult person. Does it have the same moral rights? I'm not so sure. You have to give us an argument for that. Remember – almost every cell in the human body has 46 human chromosomes. They can't all be persons.

You should also consider the fact that a child with Down syndrome has an extra chromosome. That child doesn't fit your definition.

Fred Speaking

OP COMMENT ON THE GENETIC DEFINITION

I'm a Catholic and I agree with a lot of what Diego is saying, including what he said about the importance of clear scientific evidence. The United States Conference of Catholic Bishops (USCCB) has said that "Modern genetics demonstrated that this individual [the union of a sperm cell and an egg cell] is, at the outset, distinctively human, with the inherent and active potential to mature into a human fetus, infant, child and adult." They go on to refer to "the scientific fact that a human life begins at conception" (USCCB, Respect for Unborn Human Life, *brackets added).*

Diego Speaking

MP SECULAR AND SCRIPTURAL ARGUMENTS

I'm going to stick to purely secular arguments today because, if I bring in my religious ideas, some of you are going to say that I am imposing my religion on others. That said, I want it to be clear that as an evangelical Christian I *could* argue for a broad definition of personhood on scriptural grounds. Let me give you a couple of examples of how scripture supports the very inclusive definition of personhood I just proposed. If I were talking with other evangelicals, these are the arguments I would make.

In the book of Jeremiah (1:5), God says to the prophet "Before I formed you in the womb I knew you, and before you were born I consecrated you...." To me, that means that each fully developed person, like any of us here, was a person from the time of conception. That's about as broad a definition as you can get.

I would also point out that the Bible clearly states that each human being is created in the image of God. God said "Let us make man in our image, after our likeness" (Genesis 1:26). Because we bear that image, each of us is, from the time of conception, a person of infinite value.

For me, those are strong arguments; and some of you may think that my ideas on abortion are based entirely on religious faith. But that's not true. You might think that it is only conservative Christians who are against abortion. That's not true either. There are good arguments based on scripture, but there are also purely secular arguments that have nothing to do with scripture. I have already mentioned Robert Joyce. You could also read the philosopher Phillip Devine for a view almost as conservative as Joyce's.

Ann Speaking

OP COMMENT ON SCRIPTURE

I'm not going to pretend to be an expert on the Bible, but I want to point out that Diego's interpretation of scripture is not the only interpretation. There are, for example, serious questions about when the embryo first bears the image of God. The philosopher Robert Wennberg is an evangelical Christian who has considered the same passages that Diego referred to and interpreted them differently (Wennberg, 60-65).

In my opinion, many passages in the Bible are vague or can be interpreted metaphorically. Unfortunately, that often makes it possible for people to find whatever they are looking for.

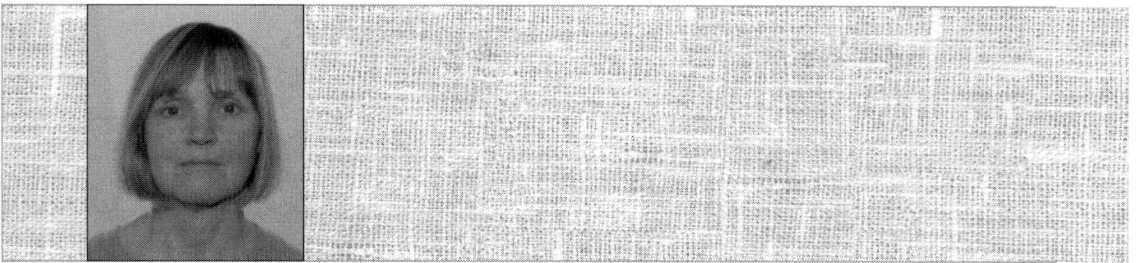

Professor Conway Speaking

QUESTIONS TO CONSIDER

We have heard several different definitions of moral personhood and moral standing. Professor Sidgwick and I have some questions we want you to think about before you accept any definition of personhood:

- Animals are alive, conscious, and they feel pleasure and pain, but we do not consider them persons. Even philosophers who believe that animals have rights do not call them persons. What's missing?

- If reasoning is crucial, then what about infants, people in comas, and those with severe intellectual disabilities?

- Must one be human to be a person? If intelligent beings from Mars landed on earth, would we consider them persons? Would you feel that they should be treated on a par with human beings? Would it be wrong to kill them? What features would they have to possess in order to be considered the moral equivalent of persons? If you had to choose between saving a human and saving a Martian from destruction, how would you decide what to do?

- If you are defining personhood in terms of chromosomes or other physical characteristics, you may be criticized for confusing biological concepts with moral concepts. Ask yourself whether we can define 'criminal' or 'saint' or 'citizen' in biological terms. If not, why not?

- Again, if you rely on counting chromosomes, consider that we had the concept of a person long before chromosomes were discovered. Talk about the natural rights of persons made perfect sense 250 years ago, but it wasn't about chromosomes. What was it about?

As you develop a definition of moral personhood, consider how it relates to the morality of abortion. Does adopting a particular definition of 'person,' even assuming we adopt it for good reasons, settle our main question about when abortion is morally right or wrong?

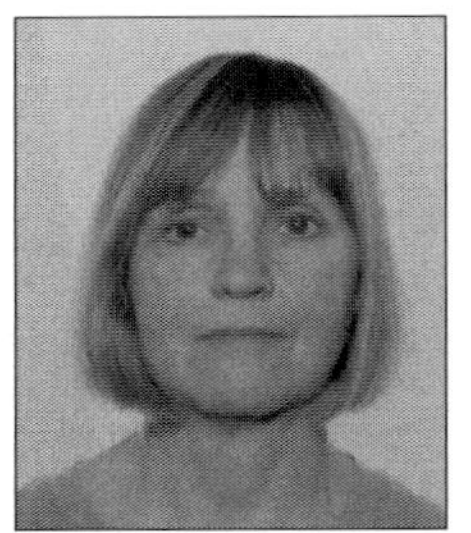

Professor Conway Speaking

OP COMMENT ON THE GENETIC DEFINITION

One more point about chromosomes and persons. It's true that the persons we meet in everyday life have 46 human chromosomes. But even so, that may not to tell us what a person is or what makes someone a person. Here's an analogy to consider:

Suppose that every lawyer (and only lawyers) wore a red carnation. The carnation would allow us to pick out the lawyers at the local court house, but it wouldn't tell us what it means to be a lawyer or what makes someone a lawyer.

In the case of lawyers, we can confirm the correlation between lawyers and carnations because we have independent criteria for identifying lawyers – things like law degrees and bar exams. In the case of persons, we need independent criteria for identifying persons that allow us to confirm the connection between persons and chromosomes. Do we have those independent criteria? What might they be?

John Speaking

ᗰ P CORE CASES AND CONTROVERSIAL CASES

I'm still undecided. Our everyday experience seems to break down into a core of cases in which we are quite sure that a moral person is present and a surrounding ring of controversial cases. Within the core, all the usual indicators are there: reasoning, use of language, self-consciousness, planning for the future, loving and hating, moral responsibility, weighing options, making decisions, and so forth. Outside the core, some of the usual characteristics are missing. Those cases include children with severe intellectual disabilities, people in comas, embryos, infants, whales, chimpanzees, and visitors from Mars.

In some cases the usual indicators of personhood were once present but are now gone (for example, people in irreversible comas). In other cases they are not now present but probably will develop (for example, embryos and infants). In still others they never appear (for example, children with certain intellectual disabilities). And in some cases (for example, whales and chimpanzees) they are present to a very modest degree but will never develop beyond that point.

Philosophers usually attempt to move from the known to the unknown. If we try to do that, can the facts about the core cases help us decide the controversial cases? I hope so, but I'm not sure.

Ayesha Speaking

MP A QUICK SUMMARY

Professor Sidgwick asked me to provide a short summary of the definitions of personhood we offered. Here it is:

- Vera offered a narrow definition that stresses cognitive behavior including reasoning, self-motivated activity, the capacity to communicate, and having a self-concept. She discounted potential as an element in personhood. Her definition is based on the ideas of Mary Ann Warren.
- I offered a definition that focused on brain activity. My definition was taken from Baruch Brody. It is considerably broader than Vera's.
- Ann offered a definition of moral standing that stressed sentience. Her definition comes from Leonard Sumner. It is broader than Vera's but narrower than mine.
- Diego offered the most inclusive definition of all. He believes that personhood begins at conception. His definition is based on the ideas of Robert Joyce, and he reinforced it with references to scripture and genetics.
- Fred, Dee, and John didn't offer definitions. John did suggest a list of characteristics that might be used to define personhood, but he admitted to being undecided about how to formulate a definition. As usual, John is confused. We all know that. I'm going to push him to say more.

Ayesha Speaking

OP COMMENT ON OUR DEFINITIONS

Philosopher Joel Feinberg has said that views on personhood divide into three groups: conservative, moderate, and liberal. The various views are on a continuum. The most conservative view holds that personhood begins at conception. The most liberal view holds that personhood develops months after birth. The moderate views fall between the two extremes. Typically, the advocate of a moderate position will hold that personhood begins at some point or phase during pregnancy such as quickening, first brain activity, the emergence of a capacity to feel pleasure or pain, or viability. It seems to me that the definitions we have proposed fall neatly into Feinberg's categories (Feinberg anthology, 3).

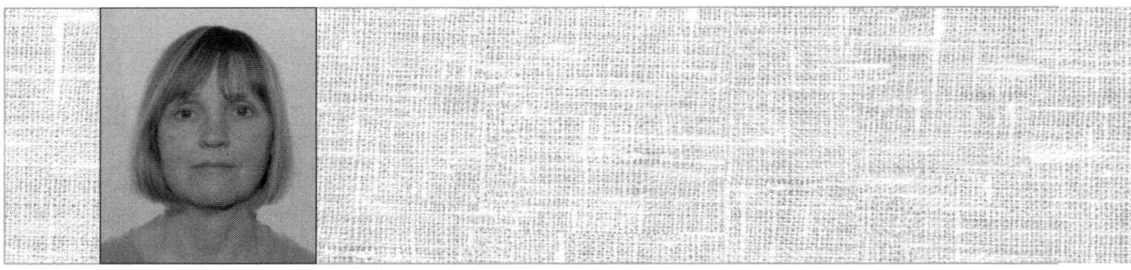

Professor Conway Speaking

MP CHANGE IN MORAL STATUS

We're going to get to some arguments about abortion in a minute. Try to keep this in mind: If your argument for or against abortion depends crucially on your definition of personhood, then you need to be able to say when (if ever) an embryo or fetus becomes a person or when its moral status changes in some way. Many pivotal points have been proposed, including the moment of conception, first brain activity, and viability.

Can you suggest why one proposal is better than the others? Can you think of other possibilities that have a better justification?

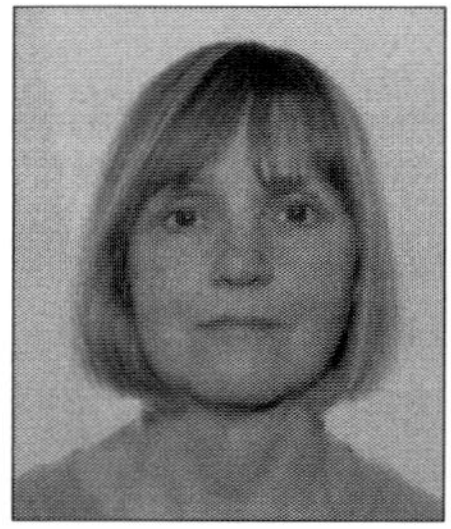

Professor Conway Speaking

OP COMMENT ON CHANGE IN MORAL STATUS

Here's a list of points at which personhood has been said to begin or when moral status changes:

- *The time of fertilization or conception*
- *The time after which dividing into identical twins is no longer possible*
- *The time when the embryo begins to bear the image of God*
- *The time when brain or heart activity can first be detected*

- *The time when the embryo or the fetus can react to stimuli*
- *The time when the embryo or the fetus can feel pleasure and pain*
- *The time of first felt movement (quickening)*
- *The time after which the fetus can live outside its mother's womb (viability)*
- *The time when the physiological basis needed for higher brain functions emerges*
- *Birth*
- *First breath*
- *Sometime after birth when the people around the infant interact with it and accept it as a member of society*
- *Sometime after birth when self-consciousness, reasoning, use of language, conscious desires, and other characteristics of fully developed people emerge*

Professor Sidgwick Speaking

MP MORAL RIGHTS

We have been talking mainly about moral persons and we have said very little about moral rights. But the point of analyzing the concept of a person is to get greater clarity on the moral status of people and what kind of beings have that same moral status. To do that, it helps to understand more about moral rights.

There are many questions about rights that are relevant to our main question about abortion. For example: What kind of a thing can have moral rights? Can rights develop gradually? How much does the potential for having rights matter?

We can't dig into all of these questions today, but I want you to be aware of them.

I thought it would be useful to introduce at least one philosopher who attempted to develop a wide-ranging view of moral rights: Joel Feinberg. I have asked John to tell us a little about his ideas. Feinberg proposed a theory of rights based on his idea of interests, but there are other theories as well.

Professor Sidgwick Speaking

OP COMMENT ON RIGHTS

Many questions about rights are similar to the questions we have asked about moral persons.

- *Instead of asking what sort of being counts as a person, we could ask what sort of being can have moral rights. What makes it possible, for example, for adult people to have moral rights?*
- *Instead of asking when (if ever) an embryo or a fetus becomes a person, we could ask when (if ever) it becomes the sort of being that can have moral rights.*
- *Instead of asking whether personhood develops gradually, we could ask whether the rights that a being has can change gradually as it develops.*
- *Instead of asking how much the potential for personhood matters, we could ask how much the potential for having rights matters.*

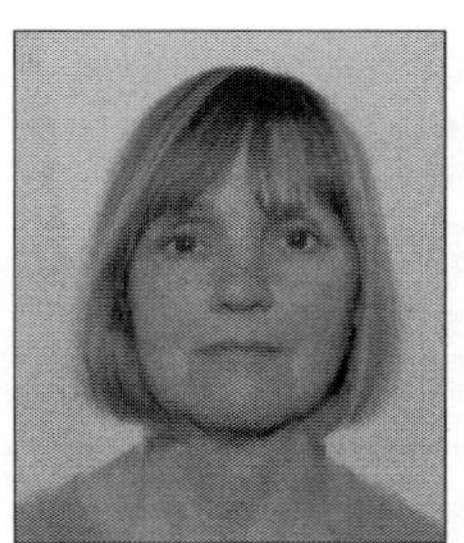

Professor Conway Speaking

OP COMMENT ON ETHICAL TRADITIONS

Everyone should realize that a rights analysis is not the only way to approach moral problems.

In addition to a rights analysis, there are other well-established ethical traditions in western philosophy.

Philosophers in the natural law tradition attempt to discover moral principles based on human nature and history. They do not always use the language of individual rights, and may define moral principles in other terms. They often say, for example, that we should do good and avoid evil, or that it is always wrong to intentionally and directly kill an innocent person. Roman Catholic philosophers often rely on natural law theory.

The utilitarian tradition concentrates on maximizing the welfare of people. For utilitarians, rights are sometimes important but never fundamental. Utilitarian morality tries to maximize the good, however it is defined. Rights are established because overall and in the long run they maximize the good. A utilitarian might ask whether it was best for a particular woman to have an abortion or whether it was best in the long run for a society to have a law restricting or allowing abortion. Many 20th-century American philosophers were utilitarians, and some still are.

The ancient tradition of virtue ethics, stemming from Aristotle, concentrates on how a virtuous person would act in various situations. There are several well-known philosophers today, including Rosalind Hursthouse and Michael Slote, working in the area of virtue ethics.

John Speaking

MP JOEL FEINBERG

Joel Feinberg (1926-2004) was an analytic philosopher who wrote about issues in moral, legal, and political philosophy. He focused on clarifying concepts and the logical relationships between concepts. In the case of rights, he asked "What *kind* of a being can have moral rights?" or "What *kind* of a being does it make sense to attribute moral rights to?"

Feinberg assumed that most of us would agree that rocks do not have rights. That isn't because we don't care about rocks. It's because a rock isn't the kind of thing that can have rights, and therefore it doesn't make sense to say that it has rights – just as it doesn't make sense to say that Saturday weighs six pounds or that the number three is blue. Saturday isn't the kind of thing that has weight and rocks aren't the kind of thing that can have moral rights.

If there are clear cases in which it makes sense to attribute rights to something (such as an adult person) and clear cases in which it does not (such as a rock), what is it that makes them different? Is it being alive, being conscious, having interests, being something that can be benefitted or harmed, being able to experience pleasure and pain, being made in the image of God, or having the potential for any of those things? It's a difficult question.

Feinberg believed that the crucial feature that identifies beings that can have rights is that they have what he called "interests." Because they have interests, they can be harmed or benefitted. If we think of a right as a device used to protect some beings from harm or to guarantee them a benefit, it follows that beings that cannot be harmed or benefitted cannot have rights and it makes no sense to attribute rights to them.

Feinberg also believed that having interests requires certain kinds of conscious activity – wants, desires, aims, and beliefs, for example. It is because rocks lack that conscious activity that they cannot have interests or rights (Feinberg 1980a, 165-168).

John Speaking

OP COMMENT ON JOEL FEINBERG

Philosopher Michael Tooley generally agrees with Feinberg's view, but he also points out that something may be the kind of thing that can have some rights but not the kind of thing that can have others. A dog is sentient, and that may make it the kind of thing that could have a right not to be tortured. But there may be other rights that require intellectual capacities that dogs lack. Perhaps for that reason a dog is not the kind of thing that can have the full rights of an adult human being.

Ayesha Speaking

MP WHAT IS A RIGHT?

I think it might be useful to say a little about the terminology philosophers use to discuss rights. I am going to suggest a few definitions, but I have to say up front that all of them are controversial.

The definition of a right. In general, we can say that a person has a right to do or to have something if and only if others have a duty not to prevent that person from doing or having that thing. In some cases, we say that a person has a right to have something (for example, medical care) if and only if someone or some institution has a duty to provide that thing to that person.

Philosophers sometimes refer to a right to do or have something without interference from others as a **non-interference right**. A right to be provided with certain goods or services is sometimes called a **welfare right**.

We can apply some of these terms to the case of abortion. Typically, those favoring abortion rights claim that a woman has a moral non-interference right to abort a pregnancy. Those opposed to abortion typically claim that a fetus or unborn child has a moral non-interference right to continue to live or at least not to be killed. Similar claims can be made about legal rights.

Ayesha Speaking

OP COMMENT ON TERMINOLOGY FOR RIGHTS

Here are some other terms that philosophers use when talking about rights:

- **Moral rights** *are established by appealing to moral principles indicating what is morally good or right or obligatory. They are not created by law or government. For example, some philosophers believe that the fundamental principle of morality is that we should maximize human welfare. They might derive moral rights from that principle.*

- **Legal rights** *or* **positive rights** *are created by government. In the United States, legal rights include both constitutional and statutory rights. Of course, we might establish a legal right to do something because we believe that people have a moral right to do that thing (for example, to marry or to have children).*

- **Human rights** *are rights that all people possess*

because of some feature or features of human beings. For example, someone might argue that human beings have certain rights because they are intelligent or sentient, because they have interests to defend, or because they can be harmed in various ways.

- **Absolute rights** *are rights that can never be justifiably abridged or overridden. Someone might claim that an innocent person has an absolute right not to be killed.*

- **Prima facie rights** *are rights "on the face of it." We acknowledge such rights under normal circumstances, but they can be overridden in some cases. We might, for example, acknowledge that a property owner has the right to keep people off her land, but also believe that this right can be overridden in cases of life and death. When deciding whether to override a prima facie right, it may be balanced against other prima facie rights or against competing moral concerns. We could also speak of prima facie obligations.*

Those are only a few of the terms associated with rights, but I hope they will help our discussion.

Professor Sidgwick Speaking

MP A STRATEGY FOR A RIGHTS-BASED ARGUMENT

Professor Conway is correct that talking about moral rights is not the only way to talk about the morality of abortion, but it is probably the most common approach here in the United States. Many people believe that the abortion controversy turns on the relationship between the rights of the child and the rights of its mother. If you want to build an argument based on rights, here's a strategy you might use:

- Decide what kind (or kinds) of beings can have rights. Why people but not rocks? What about animals, redwood trees, or landscapes?

- Decide whether human embryos, fetuses, and infants can have rights. Why or why not?
- For any of those that can have rights, decide what rights they have. What kind of a being could have a right to life? If an embryo or a fetus has a right to life, what exactly does it have a right to from its mother (or from you and me)?
- Decide what rights women have in relation to their capacity to reproduce and to control the use of their bodies.
- Decide what obligations a pregnant woman has toward her child. To what extent does that depend on her degree of responsibility for her pregnancy?
- If embryos or fetuses can have rights, how do their rights relate to the rights and obligations of their mothers?
- Look for possible conflicts, unusual circumstances, or justifications for limiting or overriding any of these rights and obligations.

Professor Sidgwick Speaking

OP COMMENT ON THE RIGHT TO LIFE

If you decide to claim that a woman or a fetus or an infant has a right to life, it will be helpful if you clarify what that means. For example, it might mean any of the following, or perhaps something else::

- *A right to any and all resources necessary to sustain life*
- *A right to specific actions or services promised by others that will help sustain life*
- *A right not to be deprived of life by anyone*
- *A right not to be unjustly deprived of life by anyone*

You might ask whether a right to life can be a matter of degree. If so, how strong is it in a given case? Are the rights to life of a dog, an embryo, a fetus, an infant, and an adult person all equally stringent? If not, why are they different?

If you decide that an embryo or a fetus has a right to life, consider whether that right automatically includes the right to support from its mother. If you wish to claim that an embryo or a fetus has a right to support from its mother, ask yourself how it came to have that right.

You might also want to ask what rights a father has in the case of pregnancy. For the sake of simplicity I have ignored that question, but you may wish to delve into it.

Professor Conway Speaking

MP LET'S MOVE ON

We've raised a lot of questions and identified a lot of things to consider when thinking about abortion. Let's move on and look at some specific moral arguments.

3.
MORAL ARGUMENTS:
For and Against Abortion

Professor Sidgwick Speaking

MP MORAL ARGUMENTS: FOR AND AGAINST ABORTION

We have heard several definitions of personhood and seen some of the questions and problems that they lead to. Now I would like to ask each of you to give us the arguments that best support your personal view on the morality of abortion.

If you rely on claims about personhood, remind us of your definition of a person. And finally, if you can connect your view of abortion with your overall moral or political philosophy, please do so.

I've asked Vera to go first. I've also asked Ayesha to give us a short summary after everyone speaks.

OK, Vera. Go for it.

Professor Sidgwick Speaking

OP COMMENT ON FRAMEWORKS

I have asked you to try to tie your views on abortion to larger ethical frameworks like utilitarianism or libertarianism or Catholic natural law for a reason. Specific moral judgments gain credibility if they can be shown to fit into a larger moral framework. If the framework unifies a lot of our specific judgments, so much the better. The combination is made more credible and more compelling.

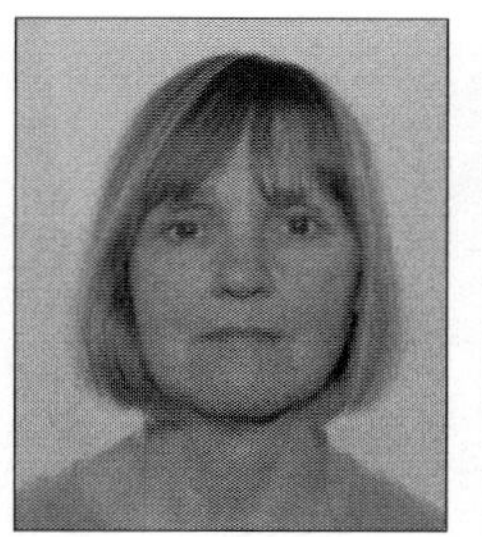

Professor Conway Speaking

OP COMMENT ON ARGUMENTS

I'd like to make a comment. It might not be necessary to have a formal definition of a moral person to make an argument about the morality of abortion. That depends on the argument you make. If, for example, you could identify one feature that a being must have in order to be a moral person, and if you could show that the embryo did not have that feature, then you could conclude that it is not a moral person. Likewise, if you could identify one feature sufficient for moral personhood and show that the embryo had that feature, then you could conclude that it was a moral person.

Vera Speaking

MP THE COGNITION ARGUMENT

I consider myself a feminist. For me that means that the interests and experiences of women are just as important as the interests and experiences of men, and I want women to be able to become everything they are capable of being. For that to happen, women must be able to control how many children they have and when they have them. As a practical matter, that means they must have the right to end an unwanted pregnancy.

I already told you about Mary Ann Warren's cognitive concept of personhood. As I said before, she believes that the traits "most central to the concept of personhood" are consciousness, reasoning, self-motivated activity, being able to communicate, and having a self-concept. It is persons who make up the moral community and have the most stringent right to life.

Without arguing that any one of these traits is necessary for personhood, she points out that the embryo and the fetus have none of them. It follows that neither the embryo nor the fetus is a person in any ordinary sense. A late-term fetus may be "somewhat more personlike" than an embryo in that it is sentient; but if it has a right to life, that right would be more like that of a "newborn guppy." It could "never override a woman's right to obtain an abortion" (Feinberg anthology, 114). The bottom line is that abortion is morally permissible in a broad range of cases.

I agree with Warren on all these points. I think she has given us a plausible analysis of personhood by identifying what it is that we value about people and hope to protect with moral rights. She has also shown what it implies in the case of abortion.

Dee Speaking

OP COMMENT ON MICHAEL TOOLEY'S VIEW

Philosopher Michael Tooley considers personhood to be synonymous with having a serious right to life. Like Warren, he argues for a very high standard for both. He believes that to have a serious right to life a being must be capable of having desires and must possess, at some time, the concept of a continuing self.

Tooley does not believe that either an embryo, a fetus, or a newborn infant has a concept of a continuing self. Therefore, it cannot have an interest in continued existence or a right to continued existence. To kill it is not a violation of its right to life because it has none (Feinberg anthology, 120-134).

Vera Speaking

OP COMMENT ON QUALITY OF LIFE

I want to emphasize something that can get lost in debates about personhood and rights and the kind of beings that can have interests – not to mention whether Martians are people. I know that this is a philosophy colloquium, and we are supposed to be discussing all of this from a very objective, very abstract point of view. I'm willing to do that here at the university, but we need to remember that we're talking about people's lives.

Whether women do or do not have access to abortion can make an enormous difference in the quality of their lives and the lives of their children. That remains true no matter what the moral status of an embryo or a fetus happens to be.

I could give you many examples of cases in which a woman's life has been turned upside down and made miserable because she was unable to end a pregnancy. And there are cases in which a child must live its whole life with severe disabilities or chronic pain.

My point is simply that if we want to make people's lives better, access to abortion is crucial. And by the way, I think that is the sort of utilitarian argument that Ann would agree with.

Diego Speaking

MP THE COGNITION ARGUMENT

Wait, Vera! If Warren is correct, then an infant is a non-person just like an embryo or a fetus. It has no right to life and infanticide is not homicide. If someone came into your home and killed your newborn child, they would not be guilty of murder. Do you really believe that?

Warren acknowledges all that. She also tell us that in our country "the deliberate killing of viable newborns is virtually never justified," but she makes it clear that killing a newborn infant is not the killing of a person. Such killing is wrong because newborns are "close to being persons," because there are usually people who are eager to care of them, and killing would deprive others of "great pleasure and satisfaction" (Feinberg anthology, 116-117).

The problem is that those considerations are completely unrelated to any rights of the infant or any harm done to the infant. Are you OK with that? I can't believe that you are. I have always believed that most pro-choice people are against infanticide. Please don't tell me I'm wrong about that.

Let me make another point. I'm not so sure that Warren is correct about a woman's rights always outweighing any rights the fetus might have. Consider the case of animals. If you believe that animals have a right not to be tortured, would you allow that right to be outweighed by even the most trivial right of a fully developed person?

Let's put the shoe on the other foot. Imagine that there were a race of superior beings. Would the rights of humans, including our right to life, always be outweighed in a conflict with their rights? I don't see why,

Diego Speaking

OP COMMENT ON INFANTS AND POTENTIAL

If you don't think that an infant is a person but you do think that infanticide is wrong because it harms the infant, then I think you should agree that potential personhood has enormous moral weight and can be the basis for a strong right to life.

But if that's true, the same could be said for an embryo or a fetus. On your own assumptions, the embryo and the fetus have the potential to become persons like any of us. I think it follows that they have the same right to live as an infant.

In my opinion, that's a good argument against what Vera and Warren are saying.

Fred Speaking

MP EMBRYOS AND RIGHTS

Vera, I agree with Diego on this. Think about what you are saying. If an embryo is not a person and has no moral rights, it seems to follow that there are no limits on what can be done to it. I can't believe you think that. Would it be all right to experiment on the embryo with drugs that would deform it? In your view, it doesn't seem to matter.

Not only that, but your view allows abortions for any reason at all. What if a woman wants to have an abortion because she doesn't want to have a girl? What if she wants to abort because she doesn't want a child with brown hair? What if she does it because she wants to take a vacation to France? You seem to be saying that she has a right to do any of those things.

Diego believes that we are developing too casual an attitude toward human life, and I think he's right. The Catholic Church has tried to develop a consistent view that includes opposition to abortion, euthanasia, and the death penalty. As a Catholic, I agree with that view.

Vera Speaking

OP COMMENT ON FRED'S CRITICISM

You're partly right, Fred. My view does allow abortion to select the sex of the child or to take a vacation to Paris, but that doesn't mean that I approve of either of those things. Sometimes people have a right to do bad things. Remember Professor Conway's distinction between the good and the right. I do believe that a woman has a right to have an abortion to select the sex of her baby, but I don't believe that's a good thing to do. In fact, I think it's terrible.

Vera Speaking

ON POTENTIAL PERSONS

I want to say something to Diego and Fred about the importance of potential personhood. I know that an embryo is a potential person. It has 46 human chromosomes and in the normal course of events it will become a person like any of us with the same right to life that we have. I understand that.

But I want you to consider a thought experiment proposed by Michael Tooley. Imagine that we could inject a drug into the brain of a kitten and as a result it would slowly develop into a person. It would eventually develop all the typical characteristics of persons including self-consciousness, desires, a vision for its future, the use of language, and so forth.

Now, assume that we have injected the drug into a kitten and the process of development has begun. Does the kitten now have the same right to life that a person has? Would it be just as wrong to kill the kitten as it would be to kill a fully developed person? I don't think so, and that seems to me to show that potential personhood carries very little moral weight.

We could say the same thing about cloning. Imagine that it becomes possible to clone human beings. Suppose we use a cell from a human finger to begin the process. If we stop the process half-way through, is it homicide? I think you would agree that it isn't.

Diego Speaking

MP THE UNIQUE VALUE ARGUMENT

Vera discounts the importance of potential, but I think she is missing something important. We all agree that embryos and fetuses are potential persons and that eventually they will become persons with a full set of human rights. Even if an embryo isn't a person, even if it doesn't have rights, it is the only thing we know of that can become a person. I think that gives it enormous, unique value. Wouldn't you agree?

I want to suggest to you that if the embryo has that value, it is reasonable to conclude that it ought not to be killed without a very good reason. Otherwise, saying that it has great value means nothing.

If you agree with that, it means that abortion on demand, even in the first few months of pregnancy, is morally wrong. There may be some abortions that are justified, but not nearly the number taking place today.

I'm just trying to defend a defenseless being that we all agree to be of enormous value. Right now, we have a virtual holocaust among unborn children. It should stop.

Professor Sidgwick Speaking

LET'S HEAR MORE

Let's hear from Ann. She has a more moderate position than Vera, but she is still fairly liberal. Then let's hear more from others.

Ann Speaking

THE SENTIENCE ARGUMENT

That's right. My view is more moderate than Vera's. I'm looking for a way to allow women to control how many children they have, but I want to avoid any view that allows infanticide or very late-term abortions. I agree with Diego and Fred on infanticide. It's not morally acceptable.

I've already said that the philosopher Leonard Sumner was interested in what he called "moral standing." If a being has moral standing, "it must be counted for something in its own right" when moral decisions are made. He also assumes that "having (some) moral standing is equivalent to having (some) right to life." (Feinberg anthology, 72).

Sumner uses "sentience," broadly defined, as a criterion of moral standing. Sentience develops gradually. There is no point at which it abruptly emerges, but there is a "threshold stage" in pregnancy during which it gradually develops. The fetus gradually acquires moral standing at the same time.

Sumner believes that the transitional stage is sometime during the second trimester of pregnancy. He concludes that abortion is morally permissible during the first trimester but requires a serious justification during and after the late second trimester. As a matter of public policy, fetal viability can serve as a rough dividing line.

Sumner's view is a middle ground between the most liberal and the most conservative views. I think it fits well with commonly-held moral intuitions and also fits into a broader utilitarian moral theory.

Ann Speaking

OP COMMENT ON UTILITARIANISM AND ABORTION

I accept a utilitarian theory of morals. Utilitarianism tells us to maximize human welfare (and maybe the welfare of animals as well). The question is whether utilitarianism can provide the basis for a reasonable view of moral status or moral standing and abortion. I think it can.

Sumner tells us that the "route from classical utilitarianism to a sentience criterion [of moral standing] is broad and plain." In his words, "All and only sentient beings are capable of having experiences that they like or dislike. All and only sentient beings, therefore, have utilities. If having moral standing means having one's utility included in the [moral] calculus, sentience must be the criterion of moral standing" (Sumner 1981, 195, 198, brackets added).

I would put it more simply. Utilitarianism emphasizes the goal of maximizing pleasure or the satisfaction of rational preferences. Any form of pleasure or satisfaction requires consciousness and the capacity to feel pleasure, pain, and satisfaction – in a word, sentience. Without sentience, the embryo or the early fetus is not something that can be benefitted or harmed. Therefore, It cannot have moral standing or rights (including a right to life) and the early termination of a pregnancy is morally permissible

Dee Speaking

OP COMMENT ON SENTIENCE

Maybe the fetus does acquire some level of moral standing as it becomes sentient. I agree that it would be wrong to cause it pain for no reason at all. But why should we think that it acquires the same high level of moral standing as an infant or an adult person? If you want to show that abortions after the fetus becomes sentient require serious justification, I think you need to show that it does occupy that high level. A low level isn't enough to prove that late abortions are permissible only for good reasons.

John Speaking

MP THE GRADUÁLIST ARGUMENT

Many people who take a moderate position on abortion believe in some kind of gradualism. According to one kind of gradualism, an embryo, a mid-term fetus, a late-term fetus, an infant, a 5-year-old child, and an adult may occupy different levels of moral standing or moral status. Progress from a lower level to a higher level is gradual. That's what Robert Wennberg believed.

I think Wennberg's view is intriguing, although he combined his gradualism with his evangelical Christianity and I'm looking for a secular approach. Like Sumner, he rejected the most extreme liberal and conservative positions and searched for a middle ground. The great strength of gradualism is that it fits with what most Americans feel about abortion; namely, that early abortions are far less serious morally than late abortions. It also implies that infanticide is wrong because it violates the rights of the infant.

In order to flesh out this idea, we may need some new concepts like the concept of a near-person or the concept of rights that are a matter of degree. Wennberg suggested that we should also begin to think about how to rank the seriousness of various reasons for having an abortion. We have an intuitive sense that some reasons are more serious than others. To have an abortion in order to take a vacation is very different from having one in order to safeguard the health of the mother. But I think we need to clarify the concept of a "more serious" reason. Does it depend on the harm to be avoided? I'm not sure. All of this is a tall order. I realize that.

John Speaking

COMMENT ON THE GRADUALIST ARGUMENT

In order to work out a gradualism something like Wennberg's, we need to develop a hierarchy of moral statuses or levels of moral standing. Then we need to show where an embryo, a mid-term fetus, a late-term fetus, an infant, a small child, and an adult fit into that hierarchy and why. The basic idea is that moral status and moral rights change gradually over time. The child's right to life begins during some phase of pregnancy and develops gradually from a weaker right to a stronger right, ending sometime after birth with the right to life of a fully developed person.

Wennberg suggested that the embryo-fetus-infant acquires a higher moral status and its right to life becomes stronger as the physiological basis needed for higher personal functions develops in the brain and the rest of the central nervous system. The result is that increasingly serious reasons are required to justify abortion. To satisfy that requirement, we need to work out a better idea of what makes some reasons more serious than others.

I think it may also be true that a woman's obligations to her child gradually increase in the course of her pregnancy (Wennberg, 112-117, 122, 170-171).

Vera Speaking

MP THE GRADUALIST ARGUMENT

I know that a gradualist view like either Sumner's or Wennberg's is attractive to a lot of people. I'm not convinced that it is the best approach, but I want to learn more about it. It allows for abortion in many cases, but it also condemns infanticide because of the harm it does to the infant. Even so, there are lots of questions to be answered.

Take Wennberg's gradualism, for example. The brain and the rest of the central nervous system develop gradually during pregnancy. But how do they supply the basis for an increasingly strong right to life? Brain development gives the fetus the potential for the traits we associate with fully developed persons, but not the traits themselves. I'm also wondering how gradualism applies to older persons who lose mental capabilities. Do they move to a lower moral status?

I know that some philosophers, including Feinberg and Philip Devine, have criticized gradualism (Feinberg 1980b, 194-197 and Feinberg anthology, 30-33). I'm not sure how to reply to what they say.

Vera Speaking

OP COMMENT ON THE GRADUALIST ARGUMENT

Ann and Sumner are saying that as the fetus gradually becomes sentient in the second trimester, it acquires moral standing; and after it has standing, the reasons needed to justify abortion become much more serious. I agree that being sentient might make the fetus the kind of thing that could have some rights. I also agree that there are reasons to believe that it has a right not to be caused pain for no reason at all. But abortion is something different. How do we get from a right to not be caused pain to a right not to be aborted without serious reasons? How serious do those reasons have to be? And how do we decide which reasons are more serious than others?

Fred Speaking

MP THE LOST FUTURE ARGUMENT

I'd like to make an argument against both Vera's view and Ann's view. I personally believe that the embryo and the fetus have the same right to life as a child or an adult like any of us here today. In that sense, they are persons. But let's assume for a moment that the unborn child isn't a person. How much does that matter?

Philosopher Don Marquis asked what it is about death that makes it wrong to kill an adult. He answered that it is wrong mainly because it deprives that adult of a valuable future – including all the "experiences, activities, projects, and enjoyments" that would have been part of that future (Marquis, 2). But that is exactly what happens to the embryo or the fetus when it is aborted. If it is wrong in the one case, it is wrong in the other. There may be some exceptions, just as there are in the case of killing an adult person, but that loss gives us a good reason to regard abortion as wrong in the great majority of cases. We could say that there is a prima facie right not to be aborted.

Notice that this argument does not assume that the unborn child is a person or that potential persons have any special importance. That's its strength.

John Speaking

OP COMMENT ON THE LOST FUTURE ARGUMENT

I think that Marquis's argument is really interesting. It is simple and seems intuitive to a lot of people. Marquis's original paper has been reprinted many times. Still, I have some questions.

First of all, I wonder what Feinberg would say about it. He asked what kind of thing could have interests and rights. We could also ask what kind of thing can suffer a loss. Does a pre-conscious embryo qualify? Keep in mind that it has no experiences or desires.

Second, philosopher Walter Sinnott-Armstrong has argued that it is morally wrong to deprive someone of a valuable future only if the loser has, and the person who deprives her does not have, a right to the necessary means to that future. I may deny you the possibility of a college education by refusing to pay your tuition, but I haven't wronged you unless you have a right to my help. If Sinnott-Armstrong is correct, we are back to trying to decide whether the embryo or the fetus has moral rights and what rights it has. In particular, we have to ask whether it has a right to a valuable future.

Ayesha Speaking

MP THE BRAIN ACTIVITY ARGUMENT

As a Catholic, I believe that most abortions are morally wrong; but unlike many Catholics, I also think that very early abortions may be permissible. Let me go back to what Baruch Brody said about being human and tell you more about his views.

Brody believed that "What is essential for being human is the possession of the potential for human activities that comes with having the structures required for a functioning brain. It is this potential that the fetus acquires at (or perhaps slightly before) the time that its brain starts functioning, and it is this potential that the newly conceived fetus does not have" (Brody 1975 114).

He adds: "In short, then, we have not reached a precise conclusion in our study of the question of when the fetus becomes a human being. We do know that it does so sometime between the end of the second week and the end of the third month. But surely it is not a human being at the moment of conception, and it surely is one by the end of the third month" (Brody 1975, 112). Brody believed that abortion after the embryo became a human being was seldom justified (Brody 1972). He did not take a position on whether it was wrong to abort a pregnancy before the embryo became a human being (Brody 1975, 119). I believe it is wrong to do so without a serious justification.

Although my church would officially disagree with Brody on when the embryo becomes a human being, I think he may be correct. To support my view I would appeal to Catholic philosophers who disagree with the official view on very early abortions. I'll say more about that later.

Diego Speaking

MP THE UNCHANGING ESSENCE ARGUMENT

It's my turn. As an evangelical Christian, I want to make a strong anti-abortion argument based on a very broad understanding of personhood. I believe that there is a scriptural basis for that understanding, but I have already said that I won't emphasize scripture here. Instead, I will rely on what Robert Joyce has said on the issue.

I have already indicated that for Joyce "Every living individual being with the natural potential, as a whole, for knowing, willing, desiring, and relating to others in a self-reflective way is a person." The embryo clearly has that potential, but it is not the potential to change into something with a different moral status. It is the potential to develop what it already is. That's key. It's something that Warren, Tooley, and Sumner would deny.

Joyce argues that nothing can develop into something essentially different from what it is. Nothing that is not a person can become a person. If the embryo grows into an adult human person, then it must have been a person from the start.

The result is that abortion is the killing of an innocent human being or person. We can argue about some difficult cases like rape and incest. I personally would allow abortion in those cases. But the conclusion in most cases is clear. Abortion is the killing of a human being and it is morally wrong.

Diego Speaking

COMMENT ON PERSONS

Theologian and minister R. C. Sproul has written that "The fetus looks like a living human person. It acts like a human person. The embryo has the genetic structure of a human person. It has the vital signs of a living human person. The fetus has sexuality and movement. With this accumulative evidence from natural science, it would seemingly require powerful evidence to the contrary to conclude that a prenatal baby is not a living human person. Why do people resist this conclusion? The answer is prejudice*" (Sproul, 62).*

Dee Speaking

COMMENT ON ESSENTIAL CHANGE

How do we know that a thing cannot become something essentially different over time? I think that Joyce is relying on brute assertion when he says that. How do we decide what counts as "essentially different"? I'm not sure I even know what those words mean. But consider this: An embryo changes from a non-conscious being into a conscious being. If that's not an essential change, what is?

Most scientists and philosophers agree that as a thing changes it may develop what are called "emergent properties." I can't think of any reason why there could not be cases in which those properties make it essentially different from what it was before. In the case of an embryo or a fetus or an infant, those emergent properties might make it a person. Why not? As a matter of fact, I think that's exactly what happens.

Here's another case to consider: A large oak tree begins life as a tiny seed in an acorn. Does it become something essentially different as it develops? It always has the same genetic structure, but its other characteristics change dramatically. Does it change "essentially"? How do we decide?

Dee Speaking

MP EXCEPTIONS

Diego, I don't see how you can make exceptions for rape and incest. You have quoted Robert Joyce, but I suspect that he would not allow those exceptions.

Why should the morally evil origins of a child justify killing it? Its origins have nothing to do with its moral status or its rights, do they?

In spite of its origins, the embryo or the fetus is innocent. If you believe that it has a high moral status, like that of an adult, how can you justify killing it when it has done nothing wrong?

Most Catholic thinkers have been consistent about this. I'll give them credit for following the logic of their position, but I'm not at all sure that you are doing the same.

Fred Speaking

OP COMMENT ON POTENTIAL

Diego, you and I agree on most of the moral issues related to abortion, but you make an exception for the case of rape. I want you to consider this: It is a terrible thing for a woman to be raped and to have pregnancy forced upon her. I agree completely with that. I also agree that her right to control her body has been violated in the worst way. But there are moral limits on what a person can do even when their rights have been violated. In the case of rape, a woman could kill the rapist in self-defense, but the case of the child is separate. She isn't justified in killing the child because her rights were violated by the rapist. The child is innocent.

Vera Speaking

MP POTENTIAL

As I said before, we do not ordinarily claim that being a potential something gives anyone the rights or the benefits of actually being that thing. Being a potential driver does not give someone the right to drive a car.

Robert Joyce tries to get around that point by claiming that an embryo only has the potential to develop what it already is. Nothing ever changes in its essence. I agree with what Dee said about that. I'm not sure what it means. It strikes me as a mysterious claim that he offers without proof.

But I'll give you this: Even though a potential person doesn't have the rights of a fully developed person, it does not follow that potential has no moral importance whatever. Diego and John may be right about that. Perhaps having potential sometimes deserves respect or special treatment. Perhaps being sentient or being a potential person gives a fetus what Sumner calls moral standing. I certainly agree that it would be wrong to torture a fetus. But that doesn't mean that it has the same moral standing or the same rights as an adult woman.

Fred Speaking

COMMENT ON POTENTIAL

I think you are being inconsistent here, Vera. How can you say that it is morally wrong to torture the fetus but morally acceptable to abort it? Doesn't killing it harm the fetus even more than torture? That's like saying that it's wrong to spank your child but perfectly all right to kill her.

Ann Speaking

MORE ON POTENTIAL

I think there are even more problems with claiming that the embryo is a person because of its potential. The potential to become a person is there. I don't deny that. If the embryo is given the right conditions, it will eventually develop into a moral person like any of us. But if the potential of the embryo makes it a person, why doesn't the potential of an egg or a sperm cell make it a person? If it is given the right conditions, it too will eventually become a fully developed moral person. Besides that, if cloning techniques improve, almost every cell in the body may turn out to be a potential person. Does that mean that all of those cells will have the moral status of an adult?

It seems to me that the extreme conservative and the extreme liberal positions both run into problems. The extreme conservative will be pushed logically to conclude that an ovum or a single-celled zygote is a person, and the extreme liberal will be pushed logically to conclude that an infant is not a person. Both of those positions are unacceptable to me and to a lot of other people. I think both of them conflict with what we might call common-sense morality.

John Speaking

m P RIGHTS AND POTENTIAL

I would like to make a few points about rights and potential based on Joel Feinberg's ideas. I already mentioned that he was interested in determining what kind of thing could have rights. He's the guy who asked why people could have rights and rocks couldn't.

His view was that only beings that had "interests" could have rights because a being without interests cannot be benefitted or harmed. He also believed that interests were "compounded" out of desires, aims, beliefs, feelings, and awareness. A being without those components could not have rights.

As far as potential goes, Feinberg insisted that being a potential person or a potential being with rights did not make something a person or a being that could have rights.

It seems to me that if we apply those ideas to an embryo, or even a mid-term fetus, we have to conclude that it does not have interests and it is not the kind of thing that can have rights. That would mean that is has no right to life.

You know that I am interested in a gradualist view of rights and moral status. I think that what I've said about rights could fit into that sort of framework and leave room for the possibility that a late-term fetus has important moral rights that we must respect.

By the way, I'm not sure whether Feinberg would agree with what I've said. There are some places where he seems to say that an unborn child is the sort of thing that can have rights and other places where he seems to say that it isn't.

Fred Speaking

OP **COMMENT ON JOHN'S VIEWS**

John, you seem to believe that an embryo cannot have rights because it does not have interests, and it cannot have interests because it lacks the necessary desires, aims, beliefs, awareness, and so on. Without those features, you say it cannot be harmed or benefitted.

It seems to me that a 5-week-old embryo has an interest in its own development, and it can be harmed by having its development curtailed. It can also be harmed if its mother drinks alcohol or takes certain drugs. It can benefit if she eats properly or takes certain vitamins. As a result, I think that it is the kind of being that can have interests and rights even though it is not yet conscious.

Dee Speaking

OP COMMENT ON RIGHTS

Remember this, Fred. Even if you could show that an embryo or a fetus is the kind of thing that can have rights, that doesn't mean that it has any particular right. It may have a right not to be caused pain or a limited right to life, but that doesn't mean that it has a right to support from its mother's body. In my opinion, that's a critical distinction.

Diego Speaking

MP THE CONTINUITY ARGUMENT

Vera and Dee reject the idea that an embryo cannot develop into an adult person unless it is a person to begin with. I disagree, but let me make a different argument. I think this is a more intuitive argument anyway.

We all agree that a full-grown adult is a person with a very strong right not to be killed. Let's work backwards from there. Moving back day by day, do we ever get to a day when we would say that we are no longer dealing with a person or no longer dealing with a being with a strong right not to be killed? I don't think that we do, and I think you would agree with me.

We can move step by step back to a newborn infant, a late-term fetus, a mid-term fetus, and an embryo. There is no way to identify a point at which the moral status of the adult person changes to some lower level and it becomes acceptable to kill it.

To be against the vast majority of abortions is simply to recognize this continuity between an embryo and an adult.

There may be some cases in which abortion is justified. I'm thinking of cases in which the life of the mother is threatened. But aside from those few cases, I think this argument proves that abortion is just as wrong as killing an adult.

John Speaking

OP COMMENT ON THE CONTINUITY ARGUMENT

I think you are making a mistake, Diego. Your argument involves what some people call the fallacy of the continuum. You are claiming that there can't be a difference in moral status between an adult and an embryo because there is no specific point at which the transition occurs. But there are lots of counterexamples. Consider the difference between day and night or between having a full head of hair and being bald. There can be very important differences without a point at which the change takes place.

Fred Speaking

MP THE CONTINUITY ARGUMENT

I want to support Diego on this. People who deny that the embryo has the moral rights or the moral status of a person have to identify some point at which it becomes a person. But, as Joel Feinberg said, "it is very difficult to find one point in the continuous development of the fetus before which it is utterly without rights and after which it has exactly the same rights as any adult human being" (Feinberg 1980b, 195). Lots of possibilities have been proposed: first brain activity, quickening, sentience, viability, birth, and more. My point is that all of them have problems. For example:

- **Brain activity** may help us to define death, but as Philip Devine points out, that only works when its loss is irreversible. In the case of a two or three-week old embryo, brain activity is absent, but it will emerge in the normal course of events. In that case, "there is no reason to regard its absence as decisive on the personhood issue" (Feinberg anthology, 38).

- **Quickening** may have a major influence on how a woman feels about her baby, but that has nothing to do with the baby's rights or its moral status.

- **Sentience** may be a reason to say it is morally wrong to cause pain to a fetus, but it will hardly supply a criterion for personhood or a high moral status. It might give the fetus a status more like that of a dog or a cat.

- **Viability** fails, as Devine tells us, because "there is no reason to suppose that the fact that a given creature cannot live outside a given environment provides a reason why depriving it of that environment should be morally acceptable" (Feinberg anthology, 39). Besides that, the time of viability is unstable. It is constantly changing with our technology. Does moral status change like that? I don't think so.

- **Birth** is just a change of location. Why would moving the newborn from the womb to a baby bed make it a person or change its moral rights?

We could consider more possibilities, but I think you get the idea. Every attempt to find a point at which the moral status of the embryo changes to that of a person runs up against serious problems. It's better to give up the search.

Dee Speaking

OP COMMENT ON CONTINUITY

Nor so fast, Fred. Philosopher Donald Vandeveer has argued that we should be careful about searching for a point in development when the embryo or the fetus becomes a person or a bearer of rights or a being with a new (and higher) moral status. There may be no such point, but it doesn't follow that an embryo has the same moral status as a late term fetus or an infant or an adult human being.

The search for the pivotal point may be a mistake, and recognizing that may require us to rephrase our question. Instead of looking for a point, perhaps we should be asking what morally significant features of the fetus appear during different stages or phases of pregnancy. And remember, we may be concerned with phases that last weeks or months.

Vandeveer also points out that although there may be no morally significant differences between the fetus in successive stages of pregnancy, there may very well be significant differences between the fetus at non-successive stages (Feinberg anthology, 68-69).

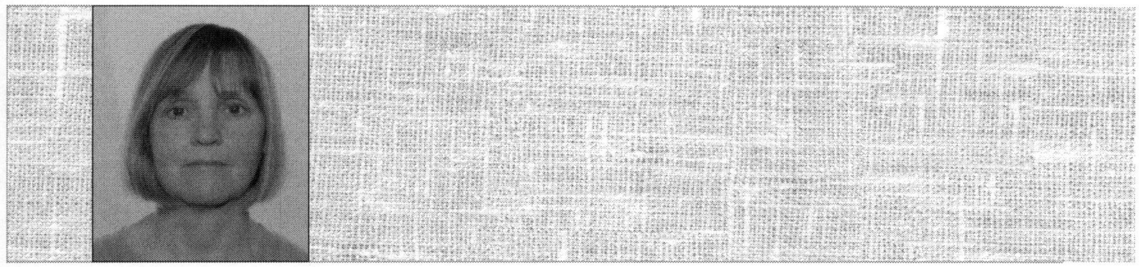

Professor Conway Speaking

QUESTIONS TO CONSIDER

We've heard arguments from everyone. Most of the arguments were based on some definition of personhood or moral standing. For those who took a broad view of personhood, I want you to think about these questions:

- The embryo or fetus lacks most of the characteristics we associate with fully developed people. Why doesn't that matter to you?
- The embryo has 46 human chromosomes. If you claim that that is a reason to grant it the same moral status as a full-grown adult, how do you support that claim? What is the connection between chromosomes and moral personhood?
- There may be no point at which the embryo or the fetus acquires moral standing or a high moral status, but some philosophers claim that there is a phase during which it gradually does so. Prior to that phase, they believe, it has no moral standing and abortion is permissible. How would you respond?

For those of you who took a narrower view of personhood, consider these questions:

- The embryo and the fetus have the potential to develop into a full-blown person. Why doesn't that matter? Is it enough to say that a potential person is not a person? If a potential person has great value, why isn't it wrong to abort it or at least wrong to abort it without a serious justification for doing so?
- Does your view allow infanticide? If you believe that infanticide is morally wrong, how do you reconcile that with your definition of personhood?

- If you believe that personhood or moral status develops gradually, how do you determine the phase or phases when it changes? Why does it change? How would you deal with criticisms of the gradualist approach? For example, Philip Devine has suggested that if personhood develops gradually before birth, it might very well continue to develop after birth. That could mean that an adult is more of a person with more rights than an infant or a three-year-old child. Do you agree with that view?
- If you took a liberal or a moderate view of abortion, how do you reply to Marquis's claim that abortion is almost always wrong because it deprives the unborn child of a valuable future?

Professor Sidgwick Speaking

MP HOW IMPORTANT IS PERSONHOOD?

You have offered several definitions of personhood and several arguments for and against abortion. You have also pointed out problems with those definitions and arguments. It may be useful at this point to recall that not all philosophers believe that the personhood or moral status of the embryo or the fetus is the pivotal issue. Perhaps our concept of personhood is not clear enough to allow us to determine whether the embryo or the fetus is a person. And even if it is, it may not settle the moral questions we are asking.

Philosopher Jane English, for example, has argued that our ordinary concept of a person includes many different elements: biological, psychological, rational, social, and legal. The way we combine the elements is subtle and does not fall neatly into lists of necessary or sufficient conditions. As a result, "a conclusive answer to the question whether a fetus is a person is unattainable" (Feinberg anthology, 153).

English also believes that even if we could determine the personhood or moral status of the fetus, it would not give us a simple answer to our main question about the morality of abortion. In her view, even if the fetus is a person, there are still cases in which abortion is morally justified. On the other hand, even if it is not a person, there are cases in which it would be wrong to kill it (Feinberg anthology, 151).

Where does that leave us? I want everyone to think about that.

Professor Sidgwick Speaking

OP COMMENT ON THE IMPORTANCE OF PERSONHOOD

English is not the only moral philosopher to question the pivotal importance of the personhood of the fetus.

Loren Lomasky does not believe that whether something is a person is crucial in determining the moral status of that thing. He also finds problems with all the usual definitions of 'person,' and concludes that "no debates over normative issues are likely to be advanced by determining whether some affected party is or is not a person" (Feinberg anthology, 161)

Beginning with the assumption that infanticide is morally wrong, he asks why it is wrong and whether there is a difference between an infant and a late-term fetus that bears on its moral status. After all, an infant can do little that a late-term fetus cannot do, and it can do little that many animals cannot do. Is there a relevant difference? He answers that "moral attributes" are "derived from social relationships" (Feinberg anthology, 171). It is the variety and density of such relationships that make a newborn infant different from a fetus and bring it into the moral community.

John Speaking

OP COMMENT ON THE IMPORTANCE OF PERSONHOOD

Let me mention one more philosopher who doesn't think that the personhood of the embryo or the fetus is crucial. I'm thinking of Rosalind Hursthouse. She's a leading figure in the area known as virtue ethics. Virtue ethics tells us to act virtuously or to act as a virtuous person would act in a given situation. The emphasis is on such virtues as honesty, benevolence, temperance, justice, and courage.

Hursthouse has applied virtue ethics to the problem of abortion; and, like the philosophers Professor Sidgwick mentioned, she believes that the moral status of the embryo or the fetus and the rights of women are largely irrelevant when deciding whether to have an abortion.

In her view, virtue ethics "transforms the discussion of abortion" (Hursthouse, 234). For example, she claims that for virtue ethics the rights of the woman are not crucial because in exercising a right a person may do something cruel, callous, or selfish. The whole point of virtue ethics is not to act that way. As a result, the approach taken by virtue ethics may reach a different conclusion than a rights-based approach in any given case.

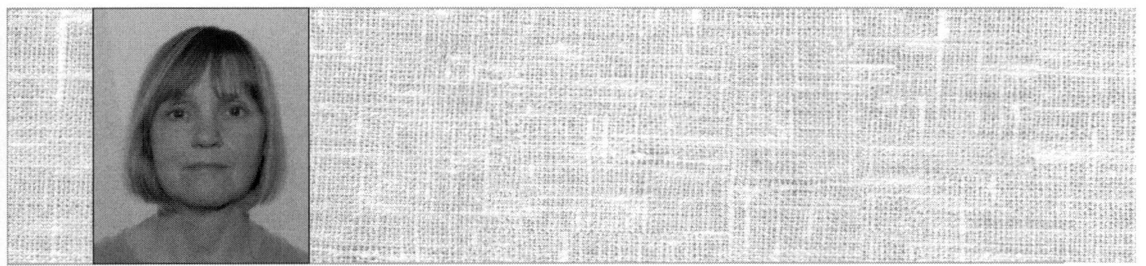

Professor Conway Speaking

MP HOW IMPORTANT IS PERSONHOOD?

I agree with Professor Sidgwick. It is not clear that deciding whether the embryo or the fetus is a person will answer our main moral question. We should at least be aware that many philosophers think that it will not.

Philosopher Ruth Macklin believes that when discussing abortion we always choose definitions of 'person' that support what we already believe about abortion. The simple fact is that "the most apparent reason for the continuing controversy, and the slim likelihood of ever reaching an agreement, . . . is that the values writers antecedently embrace determine the definition or criteria they arrive at by way of conclusion" (Garfield anthology, 81). A logical process like that will never help end the debate.

Dee Speaking

MP HOW IMPORTANT IS PERSONHOOD?

I agree that personhood may not be as important as some people think. A lot of people assume that if the embryo or the fetus is a person, then it automatically follows that to abort a pregnancy is morally wrong. Maybe it's not that simple.

Philosopher Judith Thomson proposed a thought experiment in order to refute that assumption. Suppose that a woman wakes up one day and discovers that doctors have connected her body with that of a famous violinist. The violinist needs her support for nine months and will die if he is separated from her. Would it be morally wrong for her to have the violinist disconnected from her body? He needs her support desperately, but does he have a right to it? Thomson thinks not, and I agree with her.

Professor Conway pointed out the difference between the good and the right. I think that this is a case in which it would be a very good thing for the woman to help the violinist, but she has no obligation to do so, and he has no right to her support.

Dee Speaking

OP COMMENT ON THE IMPORTANCE OF PERSONHOOD

Thomson's analogy doesn't apply to all pregnancies. It applies best to the case of a woman who becomes pregnant as the result of rape. Even so, it reminds us that the bare fact that the violinist is a person doesn't automatically settle the question whether it

> *is morally wrong to break the connection that supports him. Likewise, a woman may sometimes be within her rights to withdraw the use of her body from an embryo or a fetus even if it is a person. Since I believe in a strong principle of self-ownership, I would argue that her rights are more than sufficient to do just that in most cases.*
>
> *And by the way, I think that a modified version of Thomson's argument would make a good reply to Don Marquis's argument about the loss of a valuable future. Assume that the violinist loses a wonderful future if he is disconnected from the woman keeping him alive. I think most people would still agree that she has a right to disconnect because she did not agree to be connected in the first place.*

Ann Speaking

MP RIGHTS AND RESPONSIBILITY

It seems to me that Thomson's thought experiment with the violinist shows us two things. First, it shows that the personhood of the fetus is not always the deciding question. The violinist is a person, but the woman has a right to disconnect him from her body even if he will die. I agree with Dee on that.

Second, it shows that the responsibility that a woman bears for becoming pregnant is important when we are trying to decide whether abortion is permissible. The reason the woman in Thomson's analogy can separate from the violinist is that she is not responsible for creating the connection between them. The connection was set up without her consent.

Ann Speaking

COMMENT ON DEGREES OF RESPONSIBILITY

We should also keep in mind that responsibility is a matter of degree. Joel Feinberg has suggested the following levels of responsibility:

- *Pregnancy caused by rape (totally involuntary)*
- *Pregnancy caused by contraceptive failure, where the fault is entirely that of the manufacturer or pharmaceutical company.*
- *Pregnancy caused by contraceptive failure within the advertised 1 percent margin of error (no one's fault).*
- *Pregnancy caused by the negligence or carelessness of the woman (or the man, or both) in the use of contraception.*
- *Pregnancy caused by the recklessness of the woman (or the man, or both), disregarding the risk of pregnancy.*
- *Pregnancy caused by intercourse between partners who are genuinely indifferent at the time to whether or not pregnancy results.*
- *Pregnancy caused by the deliberate decision of the parties to have a child (completely voluntary) (Feinberg 1980b, 212).*

It may be true, as John suggested, that a fetus has a gradually increasing moral status and a gradually strengthening right to life. But that right to life doesn't automatically include a right to support from its mother. It seems to me that its right to her support (or her duty to support it) depends partly on her level of responsibility for becoming pregnant or her choice to continue a pregnancy.

Diego Speaking

OP COMMENT ON RESPONSIBILITY

Thomson's argument, if it applies at all, applies only to the case of rape. Many, if not most, women who become pregnant do so freely. They want to become mothers and they agree with their husbands that it is time to have a child.

My point is that by freely becoming pregnant a woman takes responsibility for placing a person – her unborn child – in a position of complete dependence on her support. She has placed it in a position where it can be harmed, and therefore she has a duty to prevent that harm if she can. In other words, she takes on a duty to support her child which is certainly incompatible with aborting it. It is her own choices that limit her right to withdraw her support.

John Speaking

MP PERSONHOOD: DISCOVERY OR DECISION?

Professor Conway mentioned Ruth Macklin. I want to pick up on that. I read an article by Macklin in which she raised an interesting point. What if our definition of personhood is partly a matter of *decision* rather than *discovery* (Garfield anthology, 85)?

Doesn't that put the question about personhood in a whole new light? It got me thinking. One of our questions is whether the embryo or the fetus is a member of the moral community. If that community is a human creation, then drawing its boundaries may be to some extent a human decision. Of course, if we say that the infant is in the community and the embryo is not, we should be able to offer some reason why we are making that decision. We shouldn't be entirely arbitrary, and we have to be consistent. But maybe there is no way to discover exactly where the boundary line of the community is located. Maybe we have to decide where to put it. In some cases, it may be reasonable to draw the line based at least partly on facts that have nothing to do with the moral status of the parties involved.

John Speaking

OP COMMENT ON DISCOVERY OR DECISION?

What if membership in the moral community is similar to being a citizen? In most cases, citizenship is pretty cut and dried, but there is a gray area including children of non-citizens born in a given nation, children with only one citizen parent, and children from other countries adopted by citizens. There is also the case of immigrants. Can they become full citizens? If so, what criteria will they have to meet in order to do so?

In all these cases, each government has to make a decision and draw a line. The United States, for example, grants citizenship to anyone born within its borders; but most nations don't do that. There are lots of reasons for drawing the line in one place rather than another, but the final decision is up to the government in question. My point is that there isn't a right or a wrong answer to be discovered. Is the boundary of the moral community similar?

Professor Sidgwick Speaking

MP LET'S HEAR MORE ARGUMENTS

Several of you have not said much. I know that Fred has views as a Catholic and Dee has views as a libertarian. Let's start with Fred.

Fred Speaking

MP THE OFFICIAL CATHOLIC ARGUMENT

You all know that I'm a Catholic. I want to tell you about the official Catholic view on abortion and put it in the context of the natural moral law tradition. Natural law is an attempt to show, on the basis of reason, how certain moral rules fit our nature as human beings.

A good source on the Catholic view is the Church's *Declaration on Abortion* published in 1974. You can find the same view in Pope John Paul II's encyclical *The Gospel of Life* (1995).

The *Declaration* stresses the importance of the moral law against homicide. There are good grounds for that law in scripture, in Church tradition, and in reason. Even a completely secular person can understand what reason tells us in this case. Each person has certain natural rights and the "first right of the human person is the right to life." It is morally wrong to kill an innocent human being, and human life is present from "the time that the ovum is fertilized." Any discrimination based on age or stage of life is unacceptable.

Some people will say that we do not know whether the embryo is a human being with the same rights that you and I have. But the *Declaration* offers a response to that criticism. We all agree that it is wrong to risk killing a person in cases when we are not sure whether someone is present. For example, it would be wrong to shoot into the dark if we weren't sure whether someone was there. It's the same with the embryo. If we aren't sure whether it is a person, we shouldn't take the risk. In the words of the *Declaration*, it is "a grave sin to dare to risk murder" (*Declaration*, p. 5-6).

Strictly from a moral point of view, I think the Church is correct, although as an American conservative I think that the law on abortion should be dealt with at the state level. I think the Supreme Court overreached in the case of *Roe v. Wade* (1973) when it declared the Texas law prohibiting abortion unconstitutional.

Fred Speaking

OP COMMENT ON THE CATHOLIC ARGUMENT

I want to say more about the Catholic view. I'm basing this on the writings of Diane Irving, a trained scientist and philosopher who taught at the Catholic University of America.

Irving believes that personhood begins at fertilization. She argues that all attempts to show that it begins after that point are based on incorrect science. Furthermore, attempts to separate the emergence of a biological human being from the emergence of personhood involve "the theoretical disaster of accepting that the idea or concept of a mind/body split has any correlate or reflects the real world." After fertilization, the zygote does develop, but it "doesn't become another kind of thing" (Irving 1999). Changes after fertilization are "accidental" rather than substantial. Her view sounds a lot like Robert Joyce's on this point (Irving 1993, 23,34). Diego has already referred to Joyce, another Catholic thinker.

*Irving also wrote about natural law ethics and its application to abortion. In her view, natural law is based entirely on human reason. She accepts the natural law view that "*one may never directly intend to kill an innocent human being*" (Irving 2000, 46; italics in original). She considers both the unborn child and its mother to be innocent human beings.*

Relying on the natural law principle of double effect, Irving considered when, if ever, a woman may have an abortion. She also asked when, if ever, a doctor may help the mother or her child to live by "legitimate medical" action and yet "permit or allow the other, unfortunately, to die."

The principle of double effect recognizes that an evil effect may sometimes be allowed in order to bring about a good effect. In those cases, we may be justified in performing medical procedures to save the life of a woman even if her child will die as a result. But that is possible only if certain conditions are met. The action taken must not be wrong in itself. The death of the child must not be directly intended, and it must not be the means by which the mother is saved. For example, if a pregnant woman has cancer, she may be given chemotherapy as a cure even though her unborn child will die as a result. But it is important that the death of the child is not sought and that it is not the means by which the mother is saved (Irving, 2000).

Vera Speaking

OP COMMENT ON NATURAL MORAL LAW

I'm skeptical about the whole natural law tradition. It seems to me that it tries to discover moral laws by studying human nature and the context in which we live. I don't see how that can be done. It may tell us what is prudent, but not what is morally obligatory.

The concept of a natural moral law is too vague. For example, an injunction to do good and avoid evil won't help us in controversial cases. Furthermore, there is no agreed-upon method for determining the natural law. As a result, it can be used to argue for or against almost anything.

Another problem is that natural law philosophers often tell us that the natural law is written in the hearts of men and women. But is it? Maybe those philosophers are projecting the moral ideas of their own social group onto everyone else. It seems to me that if we look around the world, we see great diversity in what people regard as morally good or bad. I'm not sure that anything more than the most general ideas is even close to being universal.

One more point. Irving believes that it is always wrong to intentionally kill an innocent human being. But is that true? I think there are cases in which innocent people pose a deadly threat to others. Someone who carries a deadly disease or someone who has gone mad and attacks others may be examples. It may be tragic, but in some of those cases killing may be justified in self-defense.

Dee Speaking

MP THE OFFICIAL CATHOLIC ARGUMENT

Fred, as someone who believes in self-ownership, I have basic problems with the Catholic view you presented. As I understand it, the Catholic view does not allow abortion in the case of rape, and it does not allow aborting the fetus when it is necessary to save the mother's life. I can't accept either of those views.

It seems to me that Thomson's argument about the violinist applies to the case of rape. Why should a woman be obliged to provide the support of her body to a child that is forced upon her?

In the other case, when the mother's life is in danger, I agree with Vera. It seems to me that when the fetus is an innocent threat a woman has a right to abort it. She has a right to defend herself.

Ayesha Speaking

MP A DIFFERENT CATHOLIC VIEW

Fred and I are both Catholics, but I already said that we take different views on early abortions. The official Catholic view claims that abortion is morally wrong from the moment of conception, but historically there have been respected Catholic thinkers who have thought differently. Father Joseph Donceel, S. J., is one of those thinkers. He taught psychology and philosophy at Fordham University for many years.

Donceel denied that the human soul is infused in the body at conception. In his words, "I do not know when the human soul is infused, when the embryo becomes human. But I feel certain that there is no human soul, hence no human person, during the first few weeks of pregnancy" (Feinberg anthology, 18). As a result, "it is not immoral to terminate pregnancy during this time, provided there are serious reasons for such an intervention" (Feinberg anthology, 19).

I'd like to make another point. The *Declaration* says that if we are uncertain whether the embryo is a human person, it would be wrong to risk homicide by performing an abortion. But this view has also been challenged by some Catholic thinkers. Carol Tauer, another Catholic philosopher, has argued that there are good arguments within the Catholic tradition for concluding that the risk of homicide does not always have the implications that the *Declaration* says it has. She believes that those arguments would allow some early abortions.

Fred Speaking

OP COMMENT ON AYESHA'S VIEW

I think that Ayesha is making a mistake by denying the full humanity of the embryo. I think all of you should check out John Noonan, a Catholic scholar who has written quite a bit about abortion and the law. Noonan put it succinctly:

"The positive argument for conception as the decisive moment of humanization is that at conception the new being receives the genetic code. It is this genetic information which determines his characteristics, which is the biological carrier of the possibility of human wisdom, which makes him a self-evolving being. A being with a human genetic code is man" (Feinberg anthology, 13).

Diego and I totally agree on this.

Dee Speaking

MP A LIBERTARIAN ARGUMENT

Professor Sidgwick asked me to give you my views on abortion and connect them with my libertarianism.

Libertarians believe in self-ownership, individual rights, and minimal government. Self-ownership means that people have the same control over themselves that they have over a piece of property like a chair or table. From that premise, we can derive a set of rights including the right to control the use of our bodies.

Like the country at large, libertarians are divided on the issue of abortion. There are those who believe that each woman is morally free to choose (or not to choose) to end a pregnancy. There are others who believe that abortion violates the moral rights of the fetus. The Libertarian Party platform affirms self-ownership and demands that the government leave the choice to abort a pregnancy up to the individual woman.

Pro-choice libertarians can support their position in several ways. In my view, self-ownership is the key principle involved. It provides the foundation for my right to control my body. I have the right to decide whether I will give my bodily support to an embryo or a fetus at any time right up to birth. That's what self-ownership is all about.

We talked about different views of personhood and moral rights. I'm not sure whether an embryo or a fetus is a person, but it certainly does not have a right to support from my body without my consent. It is a sensate being, and I will agree that it may have a right not to be cruelly treated, but that's as far as I can go. I want to emphasize that even if the fetus were a person, it would still not have a right to support from a woman's body.

I would also like to say that as a libertarian I want the government to stay out of our lives as much as possible. That implies minimal regulation of pregnancy and abortion.

Diego Speaking

OP COMMENT ON DEE'S LIBERTARIAN ARGUMENT

I just want to underscore the fact that there are anti-abortion libertarians. There is even an organization called Libertarians for Life.

Doris Gordon, the founder of Libertarians for Life, argued that human beings are moral persons from conception. She makes that claim because zygotes and embryos have the "root capacity" for reason and choice even though they do not have the "active capacity." She also denied that personhood is "developmental." It is a "constant." She argued that if personhood were developmental, then the right not to be killed would have to be developmental. That, she said, makes no sense. The right not to be killed "cannot be put on a scale of degrees." A person "is a person or not; there is no in-between moral, or even logical, class of beings" (Gordon 1999).

Since the embryo and the fetus have the same right not to be killed as an adult person, abortion is clearly not permitted.

By the way, Gordon also argued that when a woman freely becomes pregnant, she puts the unborn child in a position of dependence on her, and by doing so she acquires a duty to protect it from the harm to which she has exposed it. Think of it this way: if I put my disabled grandmother in the middle of a busy street, I would have a responsibility to protect her.

You might want to check out the Libertarians for Life website to learn more about what they believe.

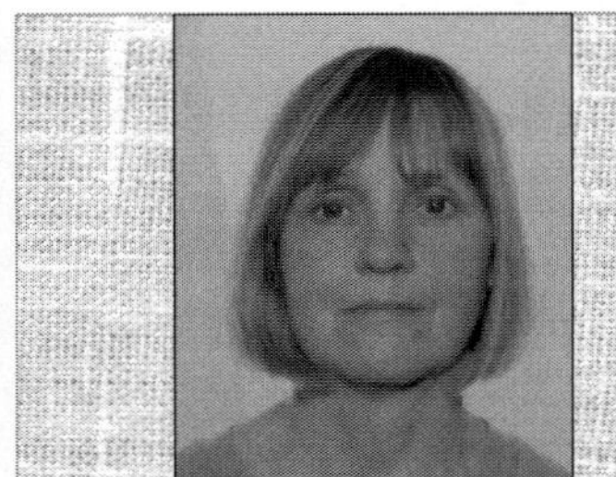

Professor Conway Speaking

MP WHAT IF WE CAN'T DECIDE?

I want to build on something John said. He's undecided about the definition of personhood and the morality of abortion. What if we can't decide the questions we've been asking?

For example, what if we can't decide whether the embryo is a person, whether it has interests or rights, whether personhood develops gradually, what the importance of potential is, whether the rights of the mother allow her to withhold the support of her body from the fetus, and all the rest?

If that is the case, would it be morally permissible (perhaps morally best) to determine the morality of abortion on the basis of other considerations such as whether the child is wanted, whether it will be healthy, whether the family's standard of living will go up or down if there is another child, whether the mother's career will be thwarted, whether the freedom to end a pregnancy allows women to achieve equality with men in general, whether the mother's health will be weakened, and so forth? Should we fall back on those considerations? I want to leave you with that thought.

I have asked Ayesha to give us a short summary of what you have said.

Vera Speaking

OP COMMENT ON WHAT IF WE CAN'T DECIDE?

My answer to Professor Conway's question is a definite "yes." I do not believe that an embryo is a person, but if there is no way to decide that question, or no way to agree on an answer, then let's make a decision about the morality and the legality of abortion based on other, more concrete, concerns. Let's look at the impact on the lives of women and children – and fathers too.

Ayesha Speaking

COMMENT ON WHAT IF WE CAN'T DECIDE?

I want to say something to Vera. Look, I know that having an unexpected child can cause problems. I also know that some children are born with serious handicaps. I've seen that happen.

But I want to point out that there are lots of cases in which an unexpected child turns out to be a boon. There are also cases in which a child with a serious handicap turns out to be a joy. You're ignoring that.

Professor Sidgwick Speaking

COMMENT ON ETHICAL ARGUMENTS

One way to approach difficult moral questions is to start with our settled judgments and try to deduce an answer. Oftentimes we can find cases that are similar enough that one case helps us to make a decision in another case. Analogies are often useful. Thought experiments like Thomson's violinist can help because they can give us a case with a clear answer that is analogous to a more difficult case.

But that approach doesn't always work. Sometimes we carefully consider our ordinary moral concepts and judgments and we still can't reach a conclusion about a difficult case. Sometimes we can't come up with a useful analogy. You need to at least consider the possibility that we are in that situation with regard to abortion. If so, what should we do?

Ayesha Speaking

MP A QUICK SUMMARY

Professor Sidgwick asked me to provide a short summary of your arguments. Here it is:

- Vera offered an argument based on a narrow concept of moral personhood that emphasizes cognitive abilities. Since the embryo and the fetus lack those abilities, they are not persons, they do not have moral rights, and abortion is morally permissible. Diego pointed out that this view implies that an infant is not a person. Therefore, infanticide would not be homicide and would not violate the rights of an infant.

- Ann offered an argument based on her beliefs as an ethical utilitarian. She relied on the views of philosopher L.W. Sumner. Sumner believes that the fetus gradually acquires "moral standing" as it becomes sentient in the second trimester of pregnancy. Abortions before it acquires moral standing are permissible. Late-term abortions require serious justifications. Vera raised a number of questions about gradualist views like those of Sumner and the evangelical philosopher Robert Wennberg.

- Fred offered an argument based on the Catholic *Declaration on Abortion* and the ideas of philosopher Diane Irving. The argument is partly based on the Catholic natural law tradition. In his view, the embryo is a person from the moment of conception. It is wrong to intentionally and directly kill it. I pointed out that not all Catholic thinkers share that view. Dee pointed out that Fred allows no exceptions for pregnancy due to rape or for cases in which pregnancy threatens the life of the mother. Fred also gave us an argument from philosopher Don Marquis that attempts to show that nearly all abortions are wrong because they deprive the embryo or the fetus of a valuable future. That argument would undercut both Vera's view and

Ann's view.

- Diego offered an argument based on the ideas of philosopher Robert Joyce. Joyce argued that a thing cannot become something essentially different from what it already is. The embryo is therefore as much a moral person as the adult it will become. Diego concludes that nearly all abortions are morally wrong, but he allows exceptions for rape, incest, and the life of the mother. Vera asked how he could justify those exceptions and suggested that he is being inconsistent. Dee questioned Joyce's claim that the embryo cannot undergo essential change.

- Dee also offered a libertarian argument based on self-ownership. She believes that a woman has a strong right to control her body and that she may withhold her bodily support from the embryo or fetus. Diego emphasized that there are other libertarians who regard abortion as a violation of the rights of the child. He also claimed that most women who become pregnant do so freely, and that by doing so they take on obligations to protect their child.

- I offered a more liberal Catholic view based on the ideas of philosopher Baruch Brody and the Jesuit priest Joseph Donceel. I believe that very early in pregnancy the embryo is not a full human person and that abortion for good reasons is morally acceptable at that time.

- John seems undecided about the nature of personhood and its importance for the morality of abortion, but he leans toward the idea that the moral status of the child and the strength of its right to life gradually increase during, and perhaps even after, pregnancy. He relies partly on the ideas of Robert Wennberg. John's view would allow early abortions but require serious reasons for late abortions or infanticide. At the same time, he admits that a lot of work needs to be done to fully develop a gradualist view. For example, we need to clarify how the development of the fetus connects with changes in its moral status. We also need to explain why some reasons for abortion are more serious and morally weighty than others.

4. ABORTION AND THE LAW

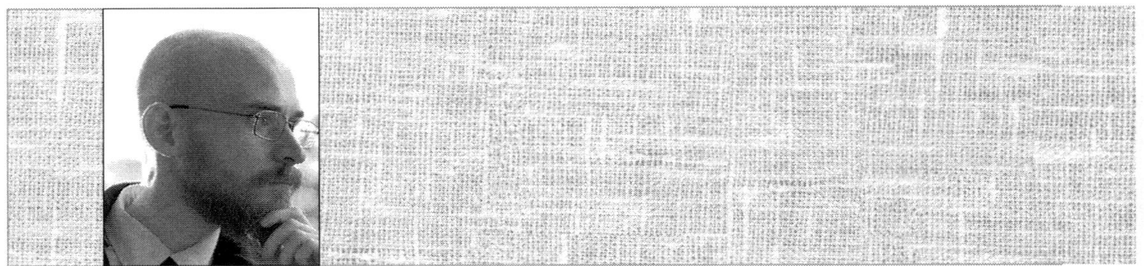

Professor Sidgwick Speaking

MP ABORTION AND THE LAW

We have heard several definitions of personhood and a series of arguments concerning the morality of abortion. Some of you connected those arguments with broader ethical frameworks like utilitarianism, libertarianism, and Catholic natural law. Now let's switch gears and talk about the connections between abortion and the law.

In some ways, questions about how the law should deal with abortion are more important than the moral questions about abortion. Our most passionate debates – the ones that bring tens of thousands of demonstrators into the streets -- are not about the moral issues but the legal ones. That's because the answers to the legal questions determine the extent to which the government will limit the availability of abortion services and punish doctors who perform abortions. To put it bluntly, the legal issues involve restriction and coercion while the moral issues do not.

Let's start with the Supreme Court case of *Roe v. Wade*. I have asked Professor Conway to tell us about it.

Professor Conway Speaking

MP *ROE V. WADE*

Thank you. The Supreme Court decided *Roe v. Wade* in 1973. It involved the case of a young woman named Norma McCorvey, a Texas resident who wanted to have an abortion. The Texas law at that time allowed abortion only to save the life of the mother. It was typical of many state laws. Corvey's attorneys argued before the Supreme Court that the Texas law was unconstitutional because it violated rights reserved to the people by the Ninth Amendment and the liberty protected by the Fourteenth Amendment.

Justice Harry Blackmun, writing for the Court in a 7-2 decision, found that the Constitution contained a right to privacy that "is broad enough to encompass a woman's decision whether or not to terminate her pregnancy." That right was fundamental but not "absolute" and it could be limited because of other state interests. As those interests became compelling, abortion could be restricted in various ways.

The Court established a trimester framework in order to balance the interests involved and to specify when state regulation was constitutional. In the first trimester of pregnancy, a woman and her physician were free to terminate a pregnancy. In the second trimester, the state was permitted to regulate abortion to protect the "health of the mother." In the last trimester, the state was permitted to impose regulations to protect "fetal life" (Schambelan, 34-36, 40-41).

As a result of this reasoning, the Texas law was declared unconstitutional. Laws restricting abortion in other states were implicitly struck down.

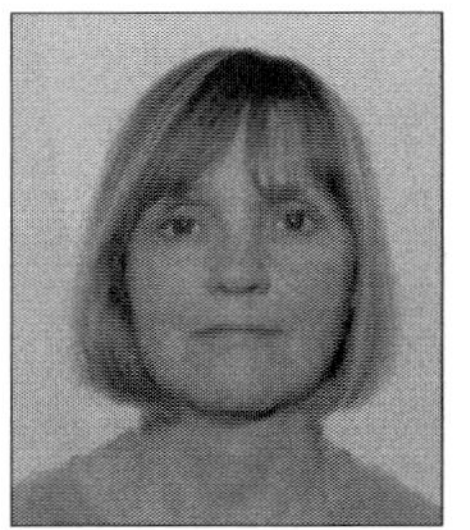

Professor Conway Speaking

COMMENT ON *ROE V. WADE*

In his decision, Justice Blackmun made some comments on the legal personhood of the fetus. He said that if the fetus were a person within the meaning of the Fourteenth Amendment, McCorvey's case "collapses" and the "fetus' right to life would then be guaranteed specifically by the Amendment." However, he went on to say that "the word 'person,' as used in the Fourteenth Amendment, does not include the unborn."

Blackmun also raised the question "when life begins," but declined to answer it. In his view, when experts in medicine, philosophy, and theology cannot agree, the Court was not in a position to speculate (Schambelan, 36-38).

Sidgwick Speaking

COMMENT ON THE SUPREME COURT

In thinking about Roe, *keep in mind that when the Supreme Court reviews a state law, its job is usually to decide whether the law is constitutional, not whether it is prudent or beneficial. In the case of abortion, for example, the function of the court is not to decide whether a state law is best for the women of that state. Its concern is with the constitutionality of the law.*

There are, of course, many different ways of interpreting the Constitution and determining constitutionality.

Fred Speaking

MP *ROE V. WADE*

As a matter of constitutional law, there have been lots of critics who believe that the reasoning in *Roe v. Wade* was flawed and that the case was wrongly decided. I'm not an expert, but I think they are right.

As an American conservative, I believe in a constitutionally limited federal government. Laws regulating abortion had been a state matter for 150 years before *Roe*. There is nothing in the Constitution that gave the federal government the right to control abortion. Not even close. That's why I believe that *Roe* was wrongly decided. It was an unwarranted intrusion into state authority. As Justice White put it in his dissent, it was an act of "raw judicial power" and an "extravagant exercise of the power of judicial review."

Fred Speaking

OP COMMENT ON *ROE V. WADE*

I think that we should all try to set aside our personal views on the morality of abortion and ask ourselves where in our political system the decision about the legality of abortion should be made. I would leave those decisions to state legislatures. Some states will be very conservative. Others will be very liberal. I don't have any problem with that, but under our Constitution the choice belongs with the states.

Diego Speaking

MP *ROE V. WADE*

I agree with Fred that *Roe* was wrongly decided. The Supreme Court overreached. The thing I want to add is that there were experts on constitutional law who criticized *Roe* and also supported more liberal laws on abortion. A person can be 100% in favor of the freedom to abort a pregnancy and still believe that *Roe* was poorly argued or wrongly decided.

Law professor John Hart Ely wrote a scathing critique of the *Roe* decision shortly after it was delivered. At the same time, he was in favor of liberal laws on abortion. Here are just a few of his criticisms.

Ely understood that an unwanted child could create enormous problems for a woman, but he suggested that those problems are properly considered by legislatures, not the Supreme Court. Second, *Roe* seemed to assume that Texas could not outlaw abortion unless it did so to protect the rights of a person, but Ely denied that assumption. Third, the Court failed to provide any reason to believe that the right to privacy included the right to terminate a pregnancy. It simply asserted that it did. It also failed to offer any reason to consider the right to be fundamental. Finally, the trimester framework assumed that the state's interest in protecting fetal life became compelling at the point of viability, but the Court did not explain why that was true.

In my view, there are many reasons to question the reasoning in the *Roe* case, and I'm not alone in thinking that.

Fred Speaking

OP COMMENT ON LEGAL PERSONHOOD

Some people seem to think that if the unborn child is not a legal or a moral person, then the law cannot protect it. I think that's a mistake.

Consider this: It is widely believed that drinking alcohol can harm an unborn child. Would it be unconstitutional for the law to prohibit restaurants from serving alcohol to pregnant women? Could the law forbid hiring pregnant women to work in environments that could do serious harm to their children? Could it prohibit prescribing certain drugs to pregnant women because they might harm the child?

It seems to me that whether the embryo is a person is irrelevant in all these cases. It is constitutional for the law to protect the child because we place value on a developing human life and we want to protect it.

Vera Speaking

MP *ROE V. WADE*

There are also legal scholars who believe that although Blackmun's reasoning in *Roe* was questionable, he reached the correct conclusion. Harvard Professor Lawrence Tribe argued shortly after *Roe* was decided that state laws like the Texas law were unconstitutional because they involve an excessive entanglement of government with religion (Tribe 1973, 25). Tribe later changed his mind about entanglement, but he offered other arguments for *Roe's* conclusion. In his book *Abortion: The Clash of Absolutes*, he claimed that "laws telling a woman she must remain pregnant deprive her of the very core of liberty and privacy." He added that if "the constitutional protection of our individual rights and human dignity means much of anything, then the freedom to decide whether or not to endure pregnancy must be deemed a fundamental aspect of personal privacy." Such a burden cannot be imposed "without the most serious justification." He found further support for his views in the equal protection clause of the Fourteenth Amendment (Tribe 1991, 104-105).

In my opinion, the most important question is not whether the reasoning in *Roe* was correct, but whether its conclusion can be supported by a sound legal argument.

Ann Speaking

OP COMMENT ON *ROE V. WADE*

To be honest, I think the people who advocate the most extreme moral positions on abortion are completely results-oriented when it comes to Roe. *Extreme liberals like Vera are going to defend* Roe *because they believe it is essential for women to be able to determine when they have children. Extreme conservatives like Diego are going to condemn* Roe *no matter what because they think it allows mass murder.*

In a situation like that, with strongly held moral values at stake, nobody really cares about the logic of the Court's decision. They want results, period. People with more moderate views find it hard to be heard.

Dee Speaking

MP *ROE V. WADE*

I believe that a woman's moral right to control her body supersedes any rights of the embryo or the fetus. As far as the law goes, Diego may be right that *Roe* was poorly argued, but it has been on the books for almost 50 years. Two generations of Americans have grown up with the idea that there is a constitutional right to terminate a pregnancy. The Court has reaffirmed the essential holding in *Roe* several times and popular expectations have formed around that fact. As a result, it should not be overturned simply because the original argument was flawed.

Fred Speaking

MP *ROE V. WADE*

I just want to remind you that *Roe* is far from being settled law. There have been critics of *Roe* since the day it was decided.

It's true that *Roe* has been around for almost 50 years, and we shouldn't take that lightly. But keep in mind that *Plessy v. Ferguson* stood for almost 60 years before it was overturned by the Supreme Court in 1954. *Plessy* was the case that held that separate but equal facilities for blacks and whites were constitutional. It too was the basis for popular expectations. Do you think it should have been upheld for that reason?

Some things are more important than popular expectations. Racial equality is one such thing. Preserving our federal system of government and protecting human life are two more. *Roe* should be overturned.

Ann Speaking

MP *ROE V. WADE*

The argument in *Roe* may not be sound, but the trimester framework corresponds roughly to what most Americans believe about the morality of abortion. They want early abortions to be treated differently, and far more leniently, than late-term abortions.

In rethinking *Roe*, I would like to combine part of what Diego said with something Vera said. I think the Court should admit that the reasoning in *Roe* was flawed but also affirm that the conclusion was sound. In place of Blackmun's reasoning in *Roe*, the Court should provide a new rationale for a woman's right to terminate a pregnancy and outline a policy along the lines of the trimester framework. The new rationale might be similar to Tribe's argument, but there may be other possibilities for the Court to consider.

Professor Conway Speaking

MP AFTER *ROE*?

The rules laid down in *Roe* have been modified over the last 50 years. In *Planned Parenthood v. Casey* (1992), for example, the Court ruled that a state could regulate abortion even in the first trimester as long as it did not impose an "undue burden" on a woman seeking an abortion. More important, the whole question whether *Roe* was well-argued or correctly decided may soon be irrelevant. With the appointment of Brett Kavanaugh and Amy Coney Barrett, the Supreme Court has shifted in a conservative direction. A draft opinion by Justice Alito was leaked to the press in May of 2022. It argues for overturning *Roe*. If the final opinion adheres closely to the draft, control over abortion may go back to the individual states.

If that happens, we are going to face a lot of questions: What sort of law should the states adopt and why? If abortion is morally wrong, should the state make it illegal? If you believe that abortion is morally wrong, are you logically compelled to support laws against it? Are you being inconsistent if you do not, or can there still be good reasons to leave the decision to the individual? How should the law deal with a moral question on which many people take radically opposed views?

Those are questions that we may have to confront all across the country.

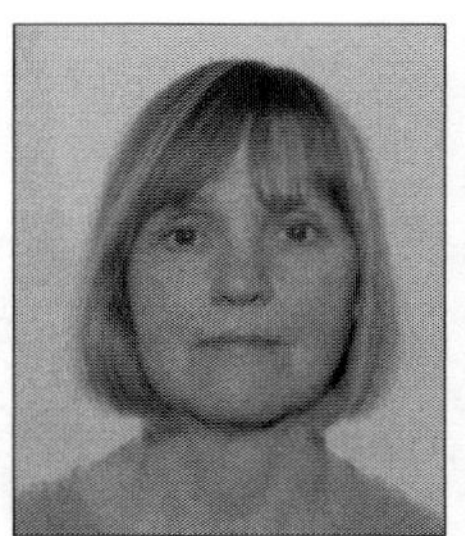

Professor Conway Speaking

OP COMMENT ON A PLURALISTIC SOCIETY

I can't help but be reminded of former New York Governor Mario Cuomo's speech at the University of Notre Dame in 1984. He argued that a Catholic governor who believed that abortion was morally wrong could and should support liberal abortion laws.

Cuomo asked what a Catholic politician should do in a pluralistic society – one including Christians, Jews, Muslims, agnostics, and others. Should he use his authority to translate his church's moral views into public policy? Cuomo answered that he should not. In his opinion, policy should be based on a "consensus view of right and wrong." Values "derived from religious belief will not – and should not – be accepted as part of the public morality unless they are shared by the pluralistic community at large, by consensus." Although he personally accepted his church's view of abortion and divorce, for example, he did not believe that he should attempt to translate those views into public policy. For one thing, it would not be feasible or workable to do so. All such decisions are matters of "prudential political judgment," not moral obligation. (Cuomo 1984)

This is not just an issue for Catholics. It's an issue for all of us. How should the law deal with abortion in a society in which so many people have very different views on the subject? It's the problem of living in a pluralistic society.

Vera Speaking

OP COMMENT ON AFTER *ROE*?

I agree that the Supreme Court may overturn Roe *soon. Right now, there is a new law in Texas that prohibits most abortions after six weeks. That's totally impractical because women often don't know they are pregnant until after six weeks.*

If that law is reviewed by the Supreme Court and found to be constitutional, it will be the end of Roe. *There will be dozens of highly restrictive laws passed all over the country. Women, especially poor women, will be trapped in situations in which there is no way to end an unwanted pregnancy. It will be a disaster.*

Diego Speaking

MP AFTER *ROE*?

I'm hoping that *Roe* is overturned. I think that would be good constitutional law and a step forward morally for our country.

I'm afraid that we have been on a slippery slope. We have legalized abortion and, in some states, assisted suicide. Why not legalize euthanasia? Why not allow parents to do away with children who are intellectually or physically handicapped?

Do we want to say, as a society, that anyone who doesn't live up to someone's idea of normality can be eliminated?

Where are we headed? Think about what we are doing. It's time to wake up!.

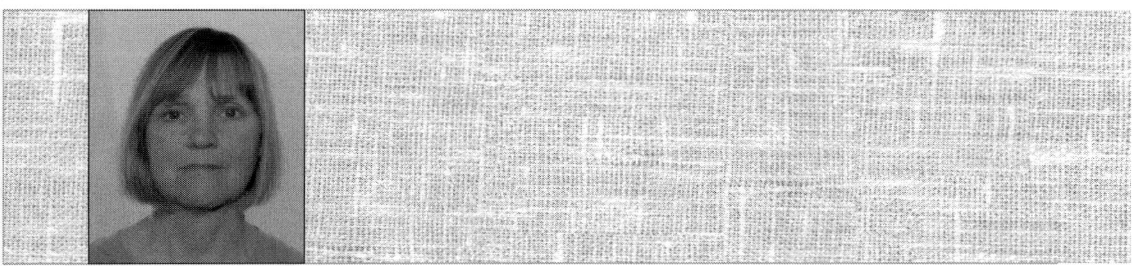

Professor Conway Speaking

MP AFTER *ROE*?

It is quite possible that the Court will overturn *Roe*. It is also possible that it will look for some sort of middle ground. Right now, for example, it is set to review a Mississippi law that prohibits most abortions after 15 weeks. If that restriction is upheld, then viability may no longer be a legal turning point so far as state regulation is concerned. On the other hand, the right to abort a pregnancy during the first 15 weeks would remain. That may not satisfy a lot of political activists, but it would not completely overturn *Roe*.

By the way, I recently read that over 90 percent of abortions occur before 15 weeks.

Ann Speaking

MP A PLURALISTIC SOCIETY

I agree with Professor Conway. We have to come to grips with the fact that we live in a pluralistic society – a society in which large groups of people hold different religious and philosophical views. We have everything from evangelical Christians like Diego to agnostics like Vera. Despite that, we need to adopt laws in order to settle disputes and avoid chaos. What should we do?

I think that Governor Cuomo was trying to address this problem in his speech at Notre Dame. Philosopher Joan Callahan (1946-2019) considered a similar problem. She agreed with Cuomo that people who believe that abortion is morally wrong can support liberal laws on abortion without being inconsistent. It was possible because there is nothing approaching a consensus on the status of the fetus and the morality of abortion. In her view, "we share a large common moral ground" and we "must begin to work from that common ground to come to an agreement on policies that can respectfully govern us all" (Baird anthology, 128).

Dee Speaking

OP COMMENT ON A PLURALISTIC SOCIETY

I'm for moderately liberal laws on abortion. That said, I recognize that Diego and Fred are sincere in their opposition. In a society like ours, with so many

> *different points of view, I keep hoping that we can find some shared political principles and values to guide us.*
>
> *At a practical level, there are some things we can all agree on. We can provide good prenatal care for women. We can provide universal medical care for mothers and infants. We can help women if they wish to give their child up for adoption. We can make it easier and less expensive to adopt a child. We can help families with the cost of raising a child.*
>
> *Most of all, we can make sure that all young women and men understand birth control and how to use it. We can make sure that birth control is available and affordable for women who want it.*
>
> *Those are things that most of us can agree on. We should look for more. Let's start talking with each other instead of shouting at each other.*

Vera Speaking

MP A HIERARCHICAL SOCIETY

Our country is pluralistic, but it is also hierarchical. Not only are there different groups with different values and beliefs, but those groups do not share power equally. There are hierarchies based on class, race, property, gender, and education.

It is also a society in which different groups have different interests and those interests often conflict. Sometimes I think that what's really going on with abortion is a good old-fashioned battle of interests, emotions, and power with a gloss of rational argument about abstractions like personhood and moral rights.

If this were a class in sociology or political science, we might be talking about different interests and how they affect our battles over abortion.

We need to keep in mind that moral and political arguments don't take place in some abstract time and place. Everyone with strong feelings about the morality or the legality of abortion occupies a specific place in society. They exercise power or they experience the power of others in ways that affect their moral and political views.

The important thing is that for the first time women are politically organized to demand the legal right to end a pregnancy.

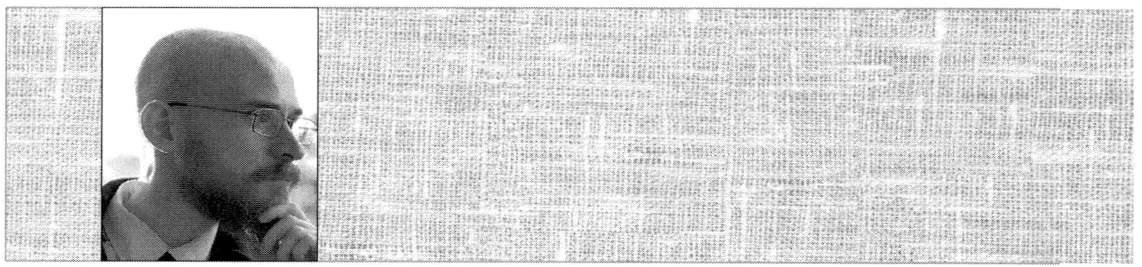

Professor Sidgwick Speaking

MP LEGITIMATE GOVERNMENT IN A PLURALISTIC SOCIETY

I'm glad that Professor Conway raised the problem of pluralism. It leads us straight to the problem of determining when a government is a legitimate government and what we have to do to have such a government. Let me explain.

By definition, legitimate governments are justified in using coercion to enforce their laws. Citizens normally have a duty to obey those laws until they can be changed.

All government rests on some principle of legitimacy, but what principle is appropriate for a pluralistic, democratic society? That's the problem of pluralism. We often say that our government is legitimate because it embodies the will of the people, but how are we to interpret that statement? For the philosopher John Rawls, it meant that law and policy should be based on shared political values and principles. That's his solution to the problem.

In the case of abortion there are deep disagreements about the nature of persons, individual rights, the importance of the Bible, and what is good for human beings. If Rawls is correct, in order to preserve legitimate government we must search for a way to determine the law on abortion on the basis of our shared values and principles. Can we do that? That's the million-dollar question.

Professor Conway Speaking

MP REDUCING THE INTENSITY OF CONFLICT

I want to add to what Ann just said.

There is a psychological aspect to the conflict over abortion in addition to the philosophical, legal, and political aspects. Each side in the conflict feels that the other side cares little or nothing about what it values most. Activists supporting liberal laws on abortion believe that people opposed to those laws care little or nothing about the hopes and dreams of liberal women. Anti-abortion activists think that the liberal activists look down on the choices made by church-going people and stay-at-home moms.

To bring down the temperature of the argument, each side must demonstrate to the other that they respect their values and their way of life. Some measures will be mainly symbolic, but others must be concrete and practical. For example, liberal support for adoption and for young, pregnant girls can help if that support is put forward out of respect for those who are opposed to abortion.

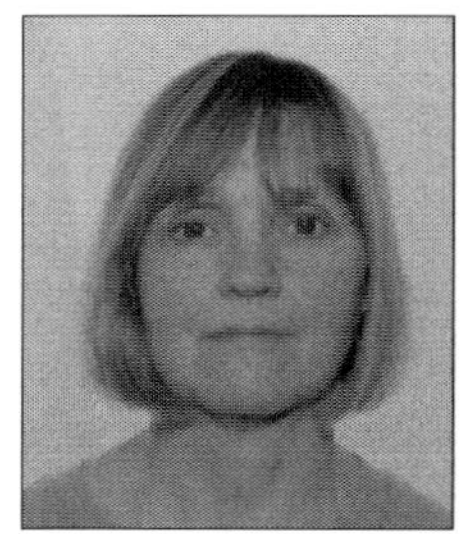

Dee Speaking

OP COMMENT ON CONFLICT

We need to understand why the conflict over abortion rights is so important to people. In my opinion, it involves a conflict between two ideas of what it is to be a woman. One idea focuses on the role of wife, mother, and homemaker. The other idea urges women to develop a broader range of capacities. Each of these ideas is of enormous importance to millions of people, both women and men. Each is deeply integrated into a way of life. Emphasizing the importance of an unborn child places value on one of those ways of life. Questioning the value of an unborn child devalues that way of life and places value on the other. That's a big part of the reason why the moral and legal differences over abortion matter so much to so many people.

As long as people feel that their way of life is being devalued by others, they will fight to defend it.

By the way, for sociological insight into the conflict over abortion rights, I recommend reading Kristin Luker's Abortion and the Politics of Motherhood.

Diego Speaking

MP A PLURALISTIC SOCIETY

Let me go back to what Ann said about making law in a pluralistic society. I agree that we should search for as much common ground as possible, and I like the list of possibilities that she offered. But I can't agree with everything she said. Of course, it would be best to make law on the basis of principles and values that we all accept. I get that. But, in this case, there are fundamental disagreements. Some of us believe that the unborn child is a moral person from the time of conception. That means that abortion is homicide, pure and simple. If someone asks me to support a liberal law on abortion because there are a lot of people with a different point of view, I'm sorry, but I can't do that. Not when a human life is at stake.

Put yourself in my shoes, Ann. Imagine that it is 1840 and the country is deeply divided over the morality and legality of slavery. Would you support a law that allowed people to choose whether to own slaves because you lived in a "pluralistic society"? Not a chance.

Vera Speaking

MP LEGAL PENALTIES

But Diego, think about the consequences of what you and Fred are saying. If terminating a pregnancy is homicide, then the woman who arranges for an abortion is a murderer. So is the doctor who performs the abortion. What choice would the law have but to treat them accordingly? It's no use saying "We shouldn't punish the woman. She has suffered enough." That's absurd. If abortion is homicide, then women who have abortions, and doctors who perform them, should be punished like other murderers. That could mean time in prison. Maybe even the death penalty. It sounds like *The Handmaid's Tale*. It's a nightmare.

I'm just pointing out the logical consequences of what you are saying. Can you live with them? If not, I think you have to change your position.

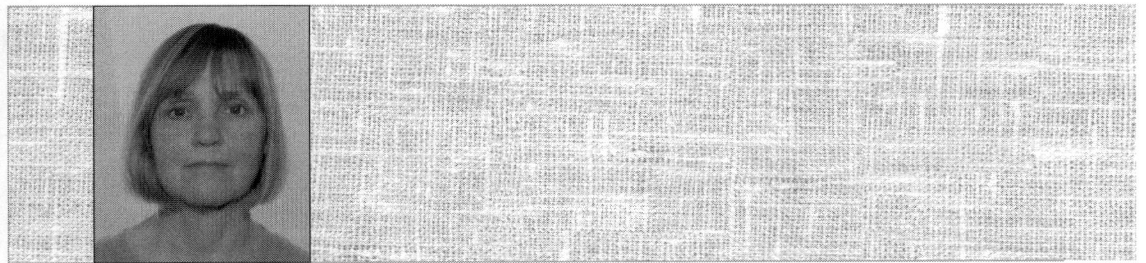

Professor Conway Speaking

MP RESTRICTIONS ON LIBERTY

I think we're groping toward a very general question about law that we need to clarify. Let me try.

One of the fundamental values in our culture is personal liberty. Yet all laws restrict liberties, and therefore they conflict with that value. That conflict gives rise to a basic question: When is government justified in imposing serious limitations on the liberties of its citizens? We aren't going to settle a general question like that today, but I want you to be aware that it hangs in the background of our discussion.

Vera has already mentioned philosopher Judith Thomson, who wrote a well-known paper on whether the personhood of the fetus is really the pivotal question in the case of abortion. Thomson wrote another paper on abortion that is less well-known. In that paper she asked when government is justified in restricting important liberties. She believed that serious restrictions were not justified when they were based on claims that it is reasonable for people to reject. She also argued that it is entirely reasonable for people to reject the claim that the embryo is a person. Therefore, legal restrictions based on that assumption were not justified.

Diego Speaking

MP RESTRICTIONS ON LIBERTY

I disagree with Thomson's idea that restrictions on important liberties are not justified if it is reasonable for some people to reject the assumptions behind those restrictions. How are we to decide whether people are reasonably rejecting those assumptions? Everybody thinks they are being reasonable when they reject somebody else's assumptions, and everybody thinks that the people who reject their assumptions are not being reasonable.

Besides that, it seems to me that there are lots of things about which reasonable people will disagree. Is Thomson saying that government is unjustified in making a choice and imposing restrictions in all those cases? In my opinion, one reason we have a democracy is that it makes decisions on those issues. That's not unjustified. That's what democracy is supposed to do.

Diego Speaking

OP COMMENT ON RESTRICTIONS

Philosopher Philip Quinn criticized Thomson's views. He asks us to consider the case of polygamy. In the 19th century, laws prohibiting polygamy imposed a serious limitation on what Mormons could do. Perhaps it would have been reasonable for Mormons to deny that monogamy was the only morally permissible form of marriage. Even so, I think we would all agree that the government was entitled to ban polygamy. The same thing is true of laws prohibiting abortion.

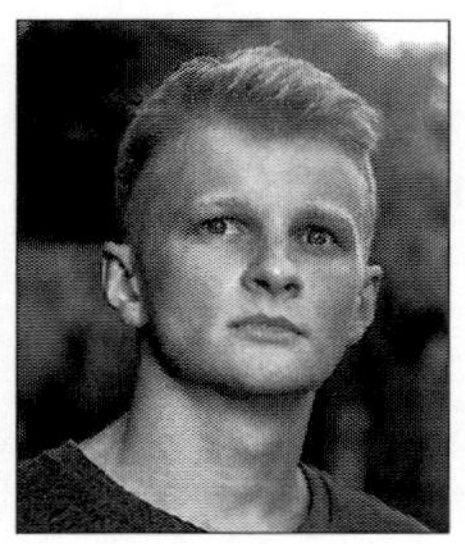

John Speaking

MP ABORTION AND THE LAW

I have been trying to develop my own view on the moral and legal issues. I want to say something about it before we move on.

I think that our questions about whether the embryo or the fetus is a person and what rights or moral status it has are really complicated. Some of the arguments seem to be based on philosophical or religious views about essential human properties, interests, personhood, personal identity, or the image of God that are not only controversial but also vague and unverifiable. As a result, I think that Thomson is correct that it is reasonable for people to reject those arguments. Other definitions and arguments seem contrived to achieve a particular result. I think that Ruth Macklin is right about that. In my opinion, the law ought not to be based on either type of reasoning. My own feeling is that the moral status and the rights of a fetus develop gradually during pregnancy. As a result, the reasons needed to justify abortion become more serious as time goes on.

I think that Diego and Professor Ely are correct that *Roe* was poorly argued. Justice Blackmun simply declared that the right to privacy includes the right to end a pregnancy. Without more argument, I am not convinced that there is a *constitutional* right to have an abortion, and that implies that state laws restricting abortion are constitutional. I also agree with Diego that an embryo or a fetus does not have to be a moral or a legal person in order for the law to protect it. But as I said, I think that the reasons usually given for adopting laws that prohibit early abortion are too vague and unverifiable. Furthermore, Thomson is right that the limitations that such laws place on women are substantial.

I interpret Thomson to be saying that the burden of proof rests on those who want to pass such restrictive laws. I think she's right, and I also think that the burden has not been met. As a result, the best thing would be for the law to leave the decision to abort early pregnancies to the women involved. Abortions late in pregnancy may be a different issue. I have to think more about that.

That's the best I can do right now, but I probably haven't made anyone happy. I can see Vera and Diego glaring at me.

5.
WRAPPING UP:
In Place of Final Answers

Professor Sidgwick Speaking

MP WRAPPING UP

Everyone has made their best arguments and taken clear positions on the questions we started with this morning. Let's try to pull things together. I'm asking each of you to do the following:

- Tell us what you think is the strongest or the weakest point in your argument.
- Tell us if there was anything important that you learned from today's discussion.
- Tell us if you have begun to rethink any part of your position or whether you have changed your mind on anything.

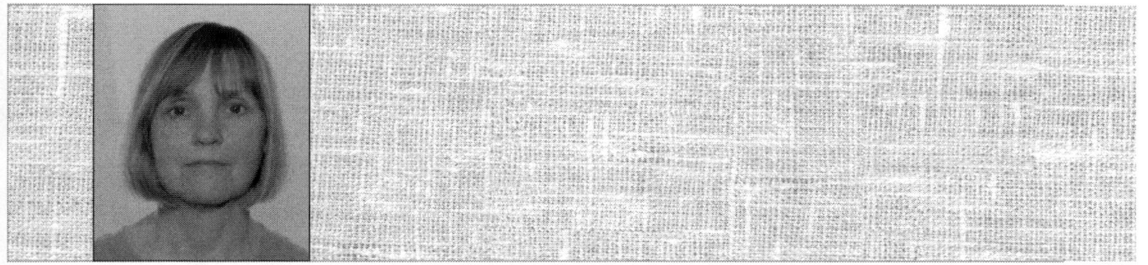

Professor Conway Speaking

MP WRAPPING UP

Feel free to make a closing statement. If you want, you can summarize your ideas and make one final plea to the group.

Tell us about your values, your main political concerns, and how they relate to abortion.

Let's get going. Vera, why don't you start? Other people can jump in after that.

Vera Speaking

MP WRAPPING UP

Look, I hope to have children myself someday when I'm ready; but I'd like to go to law school first. I love kids. I've got three nieces and nephews. They drive me nuts, but I'm crazy about them. Somebody asked me the other day if I wished that they had been aborted. I think that was supposed to be an argument against my ideas. I almost screamed at her, but I didn't. Later on, I cried. How could anybody say something like that?

What I want is full equality for women, and I believe that the availability of abortion is necessary for women to achieve that equality. We've been second-class citizens for a long time, but we finally have the power to put an end to it. Women have every right to develop *all* of their capabilities, and they should not be prevented from doing so because they can become pregnant.

The weakest part of my argument? I hate to even think about it. I accept Mary Ann Warren's view of personhood, but I think that infanticide is morally wrong. Diego nailed me on that, and maybe he's right. I have to think more about that and maybe move toward a position like Ann's or John's. Ann sees the development of moral standing as something that happens gradually in the middle of a pregnancy. She can defend early abortions and still be against infanticide. I have to think about it. I can't give you a final answer right now.

I think that one of the things I learned today is that people who are opposed to most abortions aren't just religious bigots or indifferent to the welfare of women. That includes Diego and Fred. That's good, since I like both of them.

Diego Speaking

MP WRAPPING UP

My overall concern is different from Vera's. It's not that I don't care about women. Women are just as important as men. Nothing bugs me more than someone who says that evangelicals are part of a war on women. That's not true at all. (Hey, most evangelicals *are* women.) My concern is with the moral decline of our country -- drugs, pornography, pre-marital sex, abortion, gambling, divorce, gay marriage – all of it. As I said before, I think we are going down a slippery slope.

Abortion is a big part of that decline. Millions of unborn children are being killed every year and I want it to stop. That's why I'm so opposed to *Roe v. Wade*. I'm even more opposed to the thinking that goes along with it. What is a human life worth? Sometimes it seems like we don't care at all.

I believe that an unborn child is a person from the moment of conception, and I look to philosophers like Robert Joyce and Diane Irving to support that view. I still hold to that.

Weak points? Well, I came in here thinking that the fact that an embryo has 46 human chromosomes was really important. I thought maybe that was a good way to define personhood, but now I'm not so sure. A couple of people said today that personhood is a moral concept and that it can't be defined in biological terms. Maybe that's true. I have to think more about it.

Beyond that, I've learned a lot about Vera. She's about as pro-choice as they come. I disagree with a lot of what she says, but now I can see where she's coming from. I understand her concern for women in a way that I didn't before. And I think I understand why it is so important for women to control when they have children and how many children they have. I can't condone abortion as a solution to that problem, but I want all of you to know that I am very much in favor of modern birth control. As a Catholic, Fred may disagree with me on that; but that's my view. I'm trying to protect children, not to keep women in the kitchen and force them to have babies.

Ann Speaking

m P WRAPPING UP

I agree with Vera that the legal right to end a pregnancy is important for women. My sister Carol had an abortion last year. I know what she went through, and I know how important it was for her to not have another child at that time.

I take a gradualist view of the moral standing of the fetus. It acquires moral standing as sentience slowly emerges somewhere in the middle of pregnancy. As a result, early abortions are morally acceptable and late abortions are wrong in many cases. Infanticide is certainly wrong. To put it another way, the reasons needed to justify abortion become more serious as time goes on. I think taking a gradualist view is the greatest strength of my position and I think the law should take a similar view. Early abortion should be legal and late-term abortions should require serious justification. The main concerns with late abortions should be the life and health of the mother along with serious abnormalities in the fetus.

I want to emphasize what I said before about searching for common ground that will help us to make abortion less frequent – things like counseling, adoption, birth control, and prenatal care. I have asked Diego and Fred if they want to get together and talk about the possibilities.

Fred Speaking

MP WRAPPING UP

I guess it's my turn. Morally, my position is the most conservative in the group. Like Diego, I believe that the embryo is a person from the moment of conception. I also believe, and my church teaches, that we should protect human life in all its forms. That means that abortion, euthanasia, and the death penalty are morally wrong. I may be a good political conservative, but morally I'm against the death penalty. I think one of the strengths of my position is its consistency. Human life is the most valuable thing in this world, and we have to protect it.

It's hard to be honest about the weak points in my own position. There are two things that were brought up today that are hard for me to deal with. Like Diego, I'm beginning to wonder about the significance of the fact that from conception to death a human being has 46 chromosomes. How important is that morally and philosophically? There are times when Catholic writers have put emphasis on that, but I'm not so sure now. The other thing is that I'm not at all sure what to do about legal penalties for abortion. Vera pointed out that we normally have very serious punishments for homicide. What should we do in the case of a doctor who performs abortions? And what about the woman who procures an abortion? Those are tough questions for someone who believes that abortion is the killing of an innocent human being. Our discussion today will make me think more about those issues.

Ayesha Speaking

MP WRAPPING UP

My husband and I had a baby girl last year, and I thought about having an abortion. I know how difficult that decision can be for women. Vera's right about that, but it seems to me that if we value human life, even early in pregnancy there has to be a serious reason for abortion. I didn't plan on becoming pregnant, but I didn't feel that was sufficient reason to end my pregnancy. I think it would have been wrong.

Like Fred and Diego, I think that many abortions are morally wrong, but I do have doubts about the personhood of the embryo in the first month or so of pregnancy. I've already explained that. I can accept abortion for good reasons in that early period. If I had been seriously ill when I was pregnant, I think I might have had one.

I would like us to develop more common ground and find more compromises on the political issues related to abortion. Ann has been emphasizing that, and I agree with her. I would like to ask Vera if she would consider openly supporting the current federal policy of not using government money to fund abortion. I know that doesn't fit with her political views, but it would be a great way for progressives like her to show the rest of us that they really do respect our values. I think it would help bring the country together. Professor Conway emphasized the need for mutual respect, and I think she is right.

Dee Speaking

■ WRAPPING UP

As I said before, as a libertarian I consider self-ownership to be the basis of my whole moral and political philosophy. I'm not going to budge on that. That implies extensive control over my body and a fairly broad moral right to terminate a pregnancy. The law should protect that right.

Having said that, there is something that came up today that I have to think more about. Originally, I thought that the personhood of the embryo or the fetus didn't matter much because a woman's right to control her body superseded any rights that it might have. I still think that's true in many cases – especially the case of rape or when a mother's health is seriously threatened. But Diego said that if a woman freely became pregnant, and the fetus is a person, she has taken on a duty to protect it from harm. In other words, the fetus has a right to her support. Since I'm all about protecting individual rights, I have to think more about personhood in order to decide whether I should change my views, especially on late-term abortions.

John Speaking

mp WRAPPING UP

I'm still undecided about some of the questions we have asked. Look at the list. What is a moral person? Do embryos have interests? What kind of things can have moral rights? When are state laws unconstitutional? Was *Roe v. Wade* wrongly decided? At what political level should the legality of abortion be decided? What is the proper basis for law in a pluralistic society? Wow!! And I thought differential equations were confusing.

We talked about how to define personhood and whether the embryo or the fetus is a person. It sounds to me like all the definitions lead to problems, and maybe they are all chosen to support a pre-conceived view on abortion.

In any case, I lean toward a gradualist view of moral standing. In other words, the fetus gradually develops from a very low moral status to a higher status. As time goes on it becomes sentient and develops interests and limited rights to life and humane treatment. Its rights may be less stringent than those of its mother, but they ought to be considered when decisions are made. In broad terms, that implies that early abortions are morally acceptable and late abortions require serious justification. So does infanticide. A gradual increase in moral status may continue in late pregnancy and even after birth.

I still have questions about how a gradualist view would work. Some philosophers connect the moral status of the fetus with the development of the physiological basis of higher cognitive functions. Others reject the notion that a late-term fetus has rights because it doesn't have the wants, purposes, and desires they believe are necessary for anything to have interests. I'm not sure how to reply to those concerns. I'm still trying to figure that out.

John Speaking

OP COMMENT ON WRAPPING UP

I have already said what I think about how the law should deal with abortion. The issue should be dealt with by state legislatures, and they should consider the interests of women and the values of their constituents. I think the arguments for highly restrictive laws against early abortions are very questionable. Claims that the embryo is a person seem to me to be based on vague, controversial premises that are difficult to evaluate. Sometimes the arguments are based on religious or metaphysical views that can't be verified.

I think that legislatures may have the right to make decisions based on those views, but I don't think they should. The liberty involved is too important to be restricted without better reasons. The burden of proof rests on those who want highly restrictive laws, and I do not think they have met that burden. In my opinion, there are lots of practical reasons to leave decisions about early abortions to the women involved. Those reasons have to do with health, finances, education, careers, and many other things.

Professor Conway Speaking

MP WRAPPING UP

I just want to say that I am impressed by your final statements.

The feelings you've expressed are sincere. At the same time, everyone has tried to present a clear and consistent view on the moral and legal issues we have been discussing. You've avoided a lot of the usual political rhetoric. That's no mean achievement.

Besides that, several of you have said that you heard arguments today that may make a difference in what you believe. You have a lot to think about, and you may change your mind on some things. In my opinion, that's how it should be.

Perhaps most important, I think we have all come out of the conversation today with greater respect for others and what they believe. Right now, that's what our country needs.

Professor Sidgwick Speaking

MP FINAL THOUGHTS

Well, I guess that's it. I want to thank you all for coming. You've done a great job of bringing out many of the issues and arguments concerning abortion.

I would like to throw out some final thoughts on the questions we have been discussing. These are strictly my personal opinions and suggestions. It is up to each of you to think through the arguments and reach your own conclusions.

First of all, I think we have seen that morally the issue of abortion is far more complicated than most people think. For openers, there are lots of questions about persons, rights, essential change, and moral status. The issues get technical, and a lot of hairs get split. Most of us are not accustomed to thinking about those issues and competent philosophers disagree on the answers.

Second, I think we should all practice what I would call epistemological humility. We should never mistake strong feelings for moral knowledge based on sound argument. There is a lot we do not know, and we would be wise to avoid over-confidence. Remember, it is possible that all of the most common arguments on these issues have problems. You will have to decide for yourselves whether that is true.

Third, we need to pay special attention to how the law ought to deal with abortion if we come to the conclusion that we do not know, or will never agree upon, the answers to some of the philosophical and ethical questions involved. How should that conclusion affect our actions? That is essentially the problem of pluralism that Professor Conway raised.

Assuming that the regulation of abortion goes back to state legislatures, one option is to work toward a political compromise among all groups that are genuinely concerned with human welfare. A willingness to compromise is quite different from trying to hammer through a law that reflects our personal moral view. It may seem weak or cowardly, but it may be the best safeguard against our own zeal. Keep in mind that there have been lots of people who were convinced of the moral correctness of their views but turned out to be dead wrong. Are we less fallible than they were? It may be sobering to recall Oliver Cromwell's famous plea to the General Assembly of the Church of Scotland to "think it possible you may be mistaken." How often do we ask ourselves to do that?

That's all I have to say. Thank you for coming and for sharing your thoughts.

Professor Conway Speaking

MP FINAL THOUGHTS

Let me pick up on something Professor Sidgwick just said. He suggested that there may be problems with all of the usual arguments about the morality of abortion. Feinberg believed, for example, that every definition of personhood had a "cost" where it conflicted with "moral and commonsense convictions" (Feinberg 1980b, 191). Perhaps the same thing could be said about most views on abortion.

Robert Wennberg held what he called a "gradualist" view, but he recognized that it was "not problem-free" and could not be held "with complete certainty" (Wennberg, 171). Perhaps we are all in a similar situation.

Nevertheless, we are compelled to live in the world. We must make choices and act in many ways, some of which are connected with abortion. Millions of women face a decision to abort a pregnancy or carry it to term. All of us must choose to vote for or against certain policies – or not to vote at all. Choice and action are inevitable. Unfortunately, the human condition often requires us to choose and act without certainty. There is no escape. Perhaps the best policy is to act with the humility Professor Sidgwick recommended.

Finally, I would like to go back to something I said before. In my opinion, all of us should work especially hard to demonstrate that we respect the values of those who disagree with us – no matter what side we are on. If we can show others that we respect their values, we may be able to bring greater harmony and stability out of an extremely divisive set of issues. I hope that we have shown that respect for each other today. Thank you for being here. It's been a pleasure.

ANNOTATED BIBLIOGRAPHY

Annotated Bibliography

The literature on the moral and legal aspects of abortion is large. This bibliography emphasizes the moral issues. Some of the best-known articles have been collected in anthologies. You might want to start with one of the collections edited by Baird and Rosenbaum, Cohen (and others), or Feinberg. There are also excellent full-length books on the subject. Philip Devine takes a very conservative position. Baruch Brody defends a somewhat less conservative view. L.W. Sumner takes a moderate liberal position. Michael Tooley defends a very liberal position. All of these books are clear and well-argued. The following list includes a selection of sources for you to use in developing your own views.

Anthologies

Baird, Robert M. and Stuart E. Rosenbaum, ed.

The Ethics of Abortion. Buffalo: Prometheus Books, 1989. This anthology is a collection of articles by authors on different sides of the issues.

Cohen, Marshall, Thomas Nagel, and Thomas Scanlon, ed.

The Rights and Wrongs of Abortion. Princeton: Princeton University Press, 1974. This anthology is a collection of articles by authors on different sides of the issues. It is one of the earliest anthologies on the morality of abortion and contains articles that were often reprinted later.

Cozic, Charles P. and Stacey L. Tipp, ed.

Abortion: Opposing Viewpoints. San Diego: Greenhaven Press, Inc., 1991. This anthology is a collection of articles by authors on different sides of the issues.

Feinberg, Joel, ed.

The Problem of Abortion. 2nd edition. Belmont: Wadsworth Publishing Company, 1984. This anthology is a collection of articles by authors on different sides of the issues. Feinberg has included some of the best articles written by contemporary moral philosophers.

Garfield, Jay L. and Patricia Hennessey, ed.

Abortion: Moral and Legal Perspectives. Amherst: The University of Massachusetts Press, 1984. This anthology is a collection of articles by authors on different sides of the issues. It contains extensive excerpts from Blackmun's decision in *Roe v. Wade*.

Hilgers, Thomas W., Dennis J. Horan, and David Mall, ed.

New Perspectives on Human Abortion. Frederick: University Publications of America, Inc., 1981. This anthology includes pro-life articles on medical, legal, social, and philosophical aspects of abortion. It contains an article by Robert Joyce that clarifies his views on personhood.

Noonan, John T., Jr., ed.

The Morality of Abortion: Legal and Historical Perspectives. Cambridge: Harvard University Press, 1970. Noonan was a professor of law and a circuit judge. His paper "An Almost Absolute Value in History" on the history of Catholic thinking on abortion is often cited. His views are strongly anti-abortion.

Other works

Bajema, Clifford E.

Abortion and the Meaning of Personhood. Grand Rapids: Baker Book House, 1974. Bajema develops a conservative position on abortion based partly on scriptural evidence and partly on a natural law ethic.

Brody, Baruch

"Abortion and the Sanctity of Human Life." *American Philosophical Quarterly*, Vol. 10, No. 2, (April 1973), p. 133-140.

Abortion and the Sanctity of Human Life: A Philosophical View. Cambridge: The MIT Press, 1975. Brody's book contains a discussion of philosophical issues. His approach is secular and his conclusions are largely anti-abortion.

Cuomo, Mario

"Religious Belief and Public Morality: A Catholic Governor's Perspective." 1984. Cuomo's speech is avail on the internet at https://archives.nd.edu/research/texts/cuomo.htm

Devine, Philip E.

The Ethics of Homicide. Notre Dame: University of Notre Dame Press, 1990. Devine's book is a professional philosophical treatment of the issues. He argues for a prohibition against homicide that covers infants and the unborn child from a short time after conception.

Ely, John Hart

"The Wages of Crying Wolf: A Comment on *Roe v. Wade*," *The Yale Law Journal*, Vol. 82, No. 5, (April 1973), p. 920-949. Ely criticizes the constitutional basis of Blackmun's argument in *Roe v. Wade*.

Feinberg, Joel

Rights, Justice, and the Bounds of Liberty: Essays in Social Philosophy. Princeton: Princeton University Press, 1980a. Feinberg was a professional philosopher who wrote widely on issues in moral and political philosophy. This collection of essays includes several that touch on abortion. His discussion of what kinds of beings can have rights is in "The Rights of Animals and Unborn Generations."

"Abortion" in Tom Regan, ed. *Matters of Life and Death*. New York: Random House, 1980b. Part of this article is included in Feinberg's anthology *The Problem of Abortion*.

Gordon, Doris

"Abortion and Rights: Applying Libertarian Principles Correctly." 1999. (This article is available on the internet at https://l4l.org/library/abor-rts.html. The Libertarians for Life web site can be found at https://l4l.org/index.html.)

Harrison, Beverly Wildung

Our Right To Choose: Toward a New Ethic of Abortion. Boston: Beacon

Press, 1983. Harrison is a Christian feminist theologian and philosopher. She argues that the welfare of women should be uppermost in any discussion of abortion. Her conclusions are pro-choice.

Making the Connections: Essays in Feminist Social Ethics. Edited by Carol S. Robb. Boston: Beacon Press, 1985. This collection includes Harrison's paper "Theology and Morality of Procreative Choice."

Hursthouse, Rosalind

"Virtue Theory and Abortion" in *Virtue Ethics: A Critical Reader*. Edited by Daniel Statman. Washington: Georgetown University Press, 1997.

Irving, Diane N.

"Scientific and Philosophical Expertise: An Evaluation of the Arguments on 'Personhood.'" *The Linacre Quarterly*. Vol. 60, No. 1, Article 4, (February 1993), p. 18-40.

"When Do Human Beings Begin? 'Scientific' Myths and Scientific Facts." *International Journal of Sociology and Social Policy*. Vol. 19, No. 3/4, (February 1999), p. 22-36.

"Abortion: Correct Application of Natural Law Theory." *The Linacre Quarterly*. Vol. 67, No. 1, Article 6, (February 2000), p. 45-55.

Joyce, Robert E. and Mary R. Joyce

Let Us Be Born: The Inhumanity of Abortion. Chicago: Franciscan Herald Press, 1970.

Joyce, Robert

"Personhood and the Conception Event." *The New Scholasticism*, volume 52, Issue 1, (Winter 1978), p. 97-109.

"When Does a Person Begin" in *New perspectives on Human Abortion*. Edited by Hilgers and others. See the anthology section of this bibliography. This article is adapted from "Personhood and the Conception Event" listed above.

Koop, C. Everett, M.D.

The Right To Live; The Right To Die. Toronto: Life Cycle Books, 1976. Koop was a physician and surgeon-general who wrote from an evangelical Christian perspective. His arguments are both scriptural and scientific. His position is strongly anti-abortion.

Luker, Kristin

Abortion and the Politics of Motherhood. Berkeley: University of California Press, 1985. Luker is a sociologist and professor of law. Her book is concerned with different perceptions of abortion by different groups of women. There is an informative chapter on the "world views" of activists on both sides of the issues that avoids common negative stereotypes. In this book, she takes no position on the ethical issues.

Marquis, Don

"Why Abortion is Immoral." *The Journal of Philosophy*, Vol. 86, No. 4, (April 1989), p. 183-202. (This article has often been reprinted and is available on the internet at https://rintintin.colorado.edu/~vancecd/phil215/Marquis.pdf. Page references are to the internet version.)

Mohr, James C.

Abortion in America: The Origins and Evolution of National Policy, 1800-1900. Oxford: Oxford University Press, Inc., 1978. Mohr is interested in the history, not the morality, of abortion. His focus is on the enactment of restrictive 19th-century laws at the state level. See Marvin Olasky for a different interpretation. In general, Mohr's interpretation is more agreeable to pro-choice readers than Olasky's.

Noonan, John T., Jr.

A Private Choice: Abortion in America in the Seventies. Toronto: Life Cycle Books, 1979. Noonan takes a strong anti-abortion position. He concentrates on legal precedent and advocates a constitutional amendment that would allow states to limit or prohibit abortion.

Olasky, Marvin

Abortion Rites: A Social History of Abortion in America. Washington: Regnery Publishing, Inc., 1995. Olasky criticizes many of the views held by James Mohr. In general, his interpretation is more agreeable to pro-life readers than Mohr's.

Petchesky, Rosalind

Abortion and Woman's Choice: The State, Sexuality, and Reproductive Freedom. Revised edition. Boston: Northeastern University Press, 1990. Petchesky is strongly in favor of universal access to abortion as one of several necessary conditions of women's self-determination. A selection from Petchesky is included in the Cozic and Tipp anthology listed above.

Schambelan, Bo, ed.

Roe v. Wade. Philadelphia: Running Press, 1992. Schambelan's book contains the text of *Roe v. Wade* and *Doe v. Bolton*.

Sinnot-Armstrong, Walter

"You Can't Lose What You Ain't Never Had: A Reply to Marquis on Abortion." *Philosophical Studies: An International Journal for Philosophy in the Analytic Tradition*. Vol. 96, No. 1, (1999), p. 59-72. (This article is available on the internet at https://sites.duke.edu/wsa/papers/files/2011/05/Reply-to-Marquis-on-Abortion.pdf.)

Sproul, R. C.

Abortion: A Rational Look at an Emotional Issue. Colorado Springs: Navpress, 1990. Sproul is a Christian minister. He considers both biblical and secular arguments, but his emphasis is on scripture. His position is anti-abortion.

Sumner, L. W.

Abortion and Moral Theory. Princeton: Princeton University Press, 1981. Sumner writes as a professional philosopher. He takes a moderate position that allows abortion in the first trimester but requires serious reasons to abort in the third trimester. He places special emphasis on integrating ideas about abortion into a utilitarian moral framework.

Tauer, Carol A.

"The Tradition of Probabilism and the Moral Status of the Early Embryo" in *Abortion and Catholicism: The American Debate*. Edited by Patricia Beatie Jung and Thomas A. Shannon. New York: The Crossroad Publishing Company, 1988.

Thomson, Judith Jarvis

"A Defense of Abortion." *Philosophy & Public Affairs*, Vol. 1, No. 1, (1971). This article is reprinted in the three collections edited by Cohen, Baird, and Feinberg respectively. As a philosopher, Thomson did extensive work in the area of rights. In this article, she emphasized the right of a woman to control the use of her body and challenges the assumption that if the fetus is a person, it is, by that very fact, always (or nearly always) wrong to abort it.

"Abortion: Whose Right?" *Boston Review*, Vol. XX, No. 3, (Summer 1995).

Tooley, Michael

"Abortion and Infanticide." *Philosophy & Public Affairs*, Vol. 2, No. 1, (1972).

Abortion and Infanticide. Oxford: Oxford University Press, 1985. Tooley is a professional philosopher. His book treats many issues connected with abortion. He places special emphasis on the requirements that must be met for any being to have rights, and his conclusions are pro-choice. (Articles containing the gist of Tooley's views are included in the three collections edited by Cohen, Baird, and Feinberg respectively.)

Tribe, Lawrence H.

"Forward: Toward a Model of Roles in the Due Process of Life and Law," *Harvard Law Review*, 87 (November 1973), p. 1-53.

Abortion: The Clash of Absolutes. New York: W. W. Norton & Company, 1991. Tribe is a professor of constitutional law. The book is a survey of historical, legal, and moral issues related to abortion. Tribe's position is essentially pro-choice.

United States Catholic Conference

Declaration on Abortion. 1974. This pamphlet contains a short, clear statement of the Roman Catholic position on abortion, ratified by Pope Paul VI.

United States Conference of Catholic Bishops

"Respect for Unborn Human Life: The Church's Constant Teaching. Fact Sheet by the USCCB Committee on Pro-Life Activities." (Publication available on the internet at https://www.usccb.org/issues-and-action/human-life-and-dignity/abortion/respect-for-unborn-human-life.)

Wennberg, Robert N.

Life in the Balance: Exploring the Abortion Controversy. Grand Rapids: William B. Eerdmans Publishing Company, 1985. Wennberg is a philosopher and evangelical Christian. He asks not only the questions of interest to secular philosophers, but also the related theological questions. He concludes with a moderate position. While acknowledging a woman's right to abort, he believes that more serious reasons are required as pregnancy continues. He would rely on moral persuasion to reduce the number of abortions.

Willke, John and Barbara Willke

Abortion Questions & Answers. Cincinnati: Hayes Publishing Company, Revised edition, 1988. John and Barbara Willke were trained as a physician and nurse respectively. Both had a long involvement with sex education and abortion related issues. This book and their *Handbook on Abortion* were at one time among the most widely distributed pieces of anti-abortion literature. They deal chiefly with the medical rather than the philosophical aspects of abortion.

ATTRIBUTIONS

Photo Attributions for images used in the text

All images have been cropped to fit the layout of this book.

Professor Sidgwick — photo by Chris Blonk — from Unsplash

Professor Conway – photo donated without restrictions

Ann — photo by Sean Kong — from Unsplash

Ayesha — photo by Mike Von — from Unsplash

Dee — photo by Alex Gagareen — from Unsplash

Diego — photo by Damon Hall — from Unsplash

Fred — photo by Rubén Visuals — from Unsplash

John — photo by Norbert Kundrak — from Unsplash

Vera — photo by Allison Griffith — from Unsplash

Keep Abortion Legal image — photo by Gayatri Malhotra — from Unsplash

Stop Abortion Now image — photo by Maria Oswalt — from Unsplash

ACKNOWLEDGEMENTS

I would like to acknowledge the help I received from several people in writing and publishing this dialogue. Linda Lögdberg edited the text, suggesting many improvements in clarity and consistency. Bob Moore created the image for the front cover. Alison DeLuca provided knowledge of the entire process of publishing a book at Amazon.com. Mike Denomme provided constant encouragement and advice over coffee on many Saturday mornings. Finally, my friend Peggy Morrison read the manuscript, offered many suggestions, and put up with me while I was writing. The remaining errors and limitations are entirely my own.

Made in the USA
Middletown, DE
22 May 2024